VOLUNTARY POLICE OFFICER PROGRAM VPOP

VOLUNTARY POLICE AGENT PROGRAM-VPAP

A Strategic Plan to Reclaim Haiti, Starting with Our Youth and Diaspora

A book by

BEN WOOD JOHNSON, PH.D.

Edited by

WOOD V. BIENAIMÉ, PH.D.

TESKO

TESKO PUBLISHING

www.teskopublishing.com
Middletown, Pennsylvania

The Principle of Numerical Superiority-PNS

VOLUNTARY POLICE OFFICER PROGRAM VPOP

Voluntary Police Agent Program-VPAP

A Strategic Plan to Reclaim Haiti, Starting with Our Youth and Diaspora

Prepared by:

WOOD V. BIENAIMÉ, B.S.C.J., M.A.C.J., M.A., M.P.A., PH.D.

HNP | ANTI-RIOT POLICE/CIMO | SWAT | PSU | CAT TEAM

April 2025

VOLUNTARY POLICE OFFICER PROGRAM [VPOP]

Voluntary Police Agent Program-VPAP

A Strategic Plan to Reclaim Haiti, Starting with Our Youth and Diaspora

The Principle of Numerical Superiority-PNS

(A Comprehensive Strategic Framework for Territorial Reclamation)

Prepared by Ben Wood Johnson, Ph.D. (Edited by Wood V. Bienaimé, Ph.D.)

For the Haitian National Police Leadership

Copyright © BWEC, LLC

April 8, 2025

BEN WOOD JOHNSON, PH.D.

TESKO

TESKO PUBLISHING
www.teskopublishing.com
Middletown, Pennsylvania

Eduka Editions/Tesko Publishing

This book is published in English and French. The manuscript went through a rigorous editing process.

If you want to know more about Tesko Publishing, contact My Eduka Solutions at the following address: 330 W. Main St # 214, Middletown, PA 17057, USA.

ISBN -13: 978-1-948600-92-7

ISBN-10: 1-948600-92-7

The first edition was printed and released in May 2024 (printed in the United States)

Edited by Wood V. Bienaimé (Pen name/French publications)

Format: Paperback (pbk)

Photo coverage and copyright design © 2025 Wood Oliver.

www.teskopublishing.com

Disclaimer

This document was originally compiled for the Haitian government, notably the General Director of the Haitian National Police. The information presented here is for entertainment purposes only. The views, propositions, and security strategies featured in this document are based on the author's own interpretation of the security situation in Haiti. This document does not reveal any known state secrets or other national security materials. This book reflects ideas that the author shared with several officials in Haiti while retaining intellectual authorship rights.

TABLE OF CONTENTS

EXECUTIVE SUMMARY

Haiti is under siege; the republic is in agony; the country is paralyzed. As of July 2025, it is widely understood that violent gangs, many of whom the United States declared terrorist organizations, control approximately 80 to 90% of Port-au-Prince, the capital city. Presently, the Haitian National Police (HNP) are understaffed, with an estimated of fewer than 15,000 active-duty officers.

Haitian police officers are often outmatched by the sheer mobilization capacity of local gangs to inflict incommensurable damage to the citizenry. Hope, across various communities, is fading fast, as the police institution is perceived as incapable of addressing the population's increasing security concerns. There is an urgent necessity for a different approach to national security in Haiti.

The present is a national security plan. This is a strategic document designed to reclaim Haiti. We will start by training our youth to serve the motherland. The plan starts with our youth and diaspora.

I am Ben Wood Johnson (I am also known under my French pen name, Wood V. Bienaimé). I am a person with a wealth of experience in various fields, including, but not limited to, the following: policing, public policy, public administration, public safety, and national security. I am a first generation of the Haitian national police officer program. I joined the institution since its creation in 1995. I trained at Fort Leonard Wood, Missouri. See introduction section below to learn more about me, the author.

I am also a first-generation member of the national police's first specialized units.

The Voluntary Police Officer Program (VPOP)

I am a founding member of the CIMO (anti-riot police), which includes the first Haitian SWAT team. Likewise, I am a founding member and commanding officer of the CAT Team (a specialized unit known as the Counter Ambush and Terrorism Team), an elite police unit within the national police, which was established in 1997 and primarily based in the national palace with the sole purpose of protected the Haitian president and close relatives. As will become apparent while you navigate this short technical opus, my expertise in the domain of policing, counterterrorism, and homeland security are well established.

After 30 years of law enforcement service and related academic studies, I am proposing the Voluntary Police Officer Program (VPOP) [or Option V] or (Voluntary Police Agent Program-VPAP) to help the Haitian national police restore security in the country. This proposal, in its entirety, is a Haitian-led initiative, which had been designed to break the current national safety and security stalemate. The plan will start as a pilot program. We will make adjustments as necessary or as needed. Thus, this proposition to improve security in Haiti is not a foreign fix; it is our youth and diaspora who are taking back our country.

The VPOP approach will initially recruit 200 volunteers; they will be aged between 17 and 35 years old. The goal is to help bolster the HNP's numerical superiority in the capital.

In six weeks, we will have trained the new recruits in the following areas of expertise: shooting, arrests, defense, and community policing. I will supervise the training, drawing primarily from my SWAT and CAT Team experience. The new volunteers will be deployed in Cap-Haïtien (a city of 450,000 people with moderate crime) in 2025, with seven teams covering a distance of 15 km^2 in a whole. Backed by seven vehicles and drones, they will clear gangs, hold ground, and build trust.

Haiti has been receiving international supports, namely from the MSS, which is the Multinational Security Support Mission in Haiti. However, more can be done to help restore security across the land. This plan is a step in the right direction. The goal of this initiative is a 20% crime drop across Haiti, a 70% increase in civilian trust, and gang retreat from 15 km^2 in nine months. Our success will be tracked by HNP logs and The Multinational Security Support (MSS) reports.

My understanding is that the Haitian Police can neutralize gang activities across the country. However, the best formula for police success is an increase in men power. This understanding is well understood in the literature in policing under the doctrine known as police superiority principle. My understanding of the Principle of Numerical Superiority (also known as the PNS) in policing is at the origin of the approach proposed here. This stratagem is driven by the notion of 3:1 odds, which approach beats gangs every time.

Funding for the plan will come primarily from the Haitian diaspora. We need $1 million in total from that community. Three million Haitians abroad send $4 billion yearly; $500K via crowdfunding ($100 pledges) and $500K in VPOP Bonds ($1,000 each, 3% return), which would make this security initiative and its supervised implementation [in its entirety] ours. Every dollar will be tracked. For instance:

Training ($200K)

Stipends ($360K)

Gear ($140K)

Vehicles ($200K)

Stations ($100K).

With the Haiti diaspora onboard, the implementation will be transparent. I will log on to the public monthly video reports and press releases. There will be regular press conferences for Q and A sessions about training progress in the field. The goal of this approach is to ensure transparency and accountability for every dollar we spend.

The next few chapters and pages include a comprehensive, but also detailed, written plan for the VPOP. The document is crafted based on the Police Presence Deployment Strategy (PPDS)

framework, which is a plan proposed to Haitian National Police officials in April 2025. This document aligns with the Principle of Numerical Superiority, also known as the PNS doctrine, described earlier. This edition includes a vision and mechanism for diaspora funding. It also relates to my own vision for a better approach to policing in Haiti and will depend primarily on the best mechanism to implement my recommendations.

We designed the plan as a standalone guide. The VPOP: Haiti's Hope, Our Hands, is outlined here, aimed at rallying national support and securing diaspora backing. The document is lengthy but also thorough. For clarity, I have divided it into several sections. However, the plan proposed here balances accessibility with depth.

Given my extensive background in law enforcement, the document is written in my voice. It reflects my HNP roots, training expertise, and hope-driven mission, at least as of April 7, 2025. Keep in mind that the plan is not final. It can be tweaked further.

The VPOP initiative is hope for Haiti. But it is a robust plan with strong teeth. This is a vigorous approach to help restore security in the homeland. Cap-Haïtien can be a pilot location, which will prove that the VPOP initiative works. This implementation will set the stage for the broader PPDS, which includes five phases designed specifically to reclaim Haiti from gangs and other organized criminal groups.

This approach, which is primarily based on local volunteering, will rely on Haitians and their courage to reclaim the homeland. The Haitian diaspora will invest with faith. However, the plan is not without risks, including gang pushbacks, trust gaps, and increased corruption within the national police. These are genuine security issues. Nevertheless, getting better and stronger police oversight will keep us steady.

I hope to present this plan to a wider audience. Share this document with anyone who might help turn this dream into a reality. The goal is to secure $1Million from the diaspora and another $1Million from others, notably international donors in the United States or elsewhere. A more extended goal is to initiate the pilot in Cap-Haïtien by 2026 or earlier.

If you are interested in this initiative, do contact me to join us, fund the plan, or spread this initiative. The VPOP initiative is "Fòs Nou, Espwa Nou," Our Strength, Our Hope. Let us start reclaiming Haiti from the gangs now.

Ben Wood Johnson, Ph.D.

PNH | CIMO | SWAT | USP | CAT TEAM

Former police officer

Professor of Criminal Justice and Police in America

Expert in Public Security and National Defense

INTRODUCTION: THE VISION TO IMPROVE SECURITY

As of April 2025, Haiti is in a state of chaos; the national police institution is operationally incapacitated.

Gangs continue to choke the streets of Haiti, as fear grips our homes and trust in our institutions has crumbled. With only 15,000 officers serving 11 million people, the Haitian National Police (HNP) faces significant challenges. Hover, violent gangs number around 10,000–20,000; they are armed and ruthless.

The nation finds itself in a state of political turmoil. The Transitional Presidential Council (TPC) fights, bickers, and scribbles over who should control natural resources, while Port-au-Prince burns. The Multinational Security Support (MSS) mission, though welcome, cannot fix this situation alone. With 80% of our capital lost, highways blocked, and hope fading, we find ourselves stuck.

I, Dr. Ben Wood Johnson, refuse to let Haiti die. There is a way to fix Haiti's security situation permanently. I am confident that I can help restore the motherland. See the image below.

As a first-generation Haitian national police officer, I can help make a tangible difference in restoring peace and security in Haiti. Both my technical and academic

skills could be valuable in Haiti. As the first commander of our elite Counter Ambush and Terrorism (CAT) Team, my expertise in counter assault and counterterrorism policing could help guide the Haitian police in the right direction.

1 CAT Team 1997: Commander Wood (Center)

As I have studied policing, led police-related operations, developed relevant tools, techniques, and strategies for police interventions, and watched Haiti bleed from afar, I am back with a plan to help my country. This plan is neither from the UN nor from Washington. This is plan from us, Haitians at home and abroad. The goal is to help restore the motherland.

I propose a security plan/program, which I have dubbed Voluntary Police Officer Program (VPOP) or Voluntary Police Agent Program (VPAP), to help resolve the security problem in Haiti. This plan offers a tangible solution. It is simple. We need 200 to 500 Haitian youth, aged 17–35, to volunteer to join the HNP, train for six weeks, and take back our streets, one city at a time.

The plan will be funded by our diaspora, 3 million strong people who love their country; they constantly send $4 billion home yearly. We have waited too long for a chance to fight for Haiti. Together, we will prove that numbers beat gangs, hope always beats despair, and Haitians always beat paralysis.

We can implement the program in five locations. They may include places, such as Cap-Haïtien, Jacmel, Gonaives, Hinche, or Port-au-Prince. However, our preference would be Cap-Haïtien, Haiti's second heart. We can show the world what we are made of as united Haitians. This mission is not just about the security of the nation; it is our rebirth as a nation.

ACTIVITY SUMMARY

The Voluntary Police Officer Program (VPOP) represents a critical path forward for Haiti amidst its current struggles. This initiative holds the potential to empower the youth and restore order to communities plagued by gang violence. By mobilizing the diaspora's financial resources, we can create a sustainable model that not only revitalizes the Haitian National Police but also fosters civic pride and ownership.

The proposed training will enhance the skills of young volunteers, which will instill a sense of duty and responsibility towards their communities. As these newly trained officers take to the streets, they can inspire others to join the fight against disorder.

Each city selected for this initiative will serve as a beacon of hope for Haiti, which will symbolize resilience and solidarity.

The involvement of engaged Haitians, both domestically and abroad, can cultivate a renewed spirit of collaboration. This effort could lead to a transformation in how we view security and governance in Haiti. By committing to this movement, we can forge a future where safety and trust in our institutions are restored. The VPOP initiative offers a vision, not just for survival, but for a robust revitalization of Haitian society. Our collective action can lay a foundation for a safer, more united nation for generations to come.

RECOMMENDATIONS AND OUTLINE

Below is a structured outline of the section and the ideas proposed here. This outline is specific to this chapter and includes only the main points and arguments.

Introduction: The Vision and Activity Summary

- I. Context and Problem Statement

A. Current State of Chaos in Haiti (as of April 2025)

- National Police (HNP) operationally incapacitated
- Gang control over the streets; public fear and institutional distrust
- Police force is vastly outnumbered (15,000 officers vs. 10,000–20,000 gang members)
- Political instability and dysfunction of the Transitional Presidential Council (TPC)
- Economic paralysis: blocked highways, burning capital, and fading hope

B. Ineffectiveness of External Assistance

- MSS mission welcomed.[1]
  - However, the MSS mission is insufficient to solve the security crisis alone

---

- II. Author's Background and Credibility

A. Personal Commitment to Haiti

- Author (Dr. Johnson) has a lengthy professional experience. He is a first-generation HNP officer

---

[1] The Multinational Security Support (MSS) is described as a UN-mandated mission in Haiti. The police-med force is led by Kenya. The mission was designed to help Haiti's police force restore security. Another goal is to combat rampant gang violence. The mission was established in October 2023. It was subsequently renewed by the UN Security Council. The mission aims to curb violence, facilitate humanitarian aid, and create conditions for free and fair elections. However, the results have been scarce.

- Trained in the U.S

- He is specialized in anti-riot and counterterrorism

- Former commander in elite HNP units

- He returned to Haiti with a self-initiated plan

- III. Proposed Solution: Voluntary Police Officer Program (VPOP)

A. Core Idea

- Recruit 200–500 Haitian youth (ages 17–35)

- Six-week training program to prepare volunteers for police service

- Goal: reclaim cities from gang control, one by one

B. Funding Source

- Mobilize financial support from the Haitian diaspora (approx. 3 million members)

- Capitalize on the existing $4 billion annual remittances to fund the program

C. Pilot Locations

- Cap-Haïtien was preferred as the starting point

- Other possible cities: Jacmel, Gonaives, Hinche, Port-au-Prince

---

- IV. Program Vision and Broader Impacts

A. Youth Empowerment

- Provide direction and purpose to young Haitians

- Create civic responsibility and local ownership of public safety

B. Revitalization of National Institutions

- Strengthen and restore public trust in HNP

- Demonstrate that collective Haitian action can overcome the crisis

C. Symbolism and Replication

- Each participating city as a "beacon of hope" and model of resilience

- Long-term vision for national rebirth and security transformation

---

- V. Call to Action

- Emphasis on Haitian unity and determination

- Rejection of passivity and foreign dependency

- Framing the VPOP initiative as a historic opportunity for national revival

Note: The concept of Voluntary Police Officer Program (VPOP) or Voluntary Police Agent Program-VPAP can also be understood [in French] as Programme d'agents de police volontaires (PAPV) or Programme d'officiers de police volontaires (POPV).

WHY THE VPOP/PAPV, WHY NOW?

I have spent the last 30 years learning how to protect Haiti. I started in the medical field. However, I quickly realized that my call was not in medicine. I was born to heal souls, not bodies. Currently, Haiti's soul is dying. There is a need to save the homeland.

In police matters, both in the U.S. and elsewhere across the globe, one truth stands out: numbers always win. I understand that philosophical approach. I have ostensibly made it my philosophy in the way I address law enforcement. Over the years, I have developed several security materials and documents that emphasized the doctrine of police superiority.

My Police Presence Deployment Strategy (PPDS) calls this approach the Principle of Numerical Superiority (PNS). The goal is to help the Haitian National

Police (HNP) reclaim lost territories from gangs. The problem is that the HNP is presently understaffed. Police officers are not performing at their maximum capacity.

We can restore the HNP's ability to serve and protect the citizens. The police must outnumber the gangs 3-to-1, not limp along at 1.36 officers per 1,000 people. In stable places, a ratio of 2.5 officers per 1,000 people is effective. However, in Haiti's current security chaos, we need 4–5 officers, especially in gang zones. When there is no police presence or when law enforcement is overburdened, gangs thrive. The VPOP approach will make the HNP thick and will help embolden police presence, which will help in police operations across gang-controlled places.

Why now? It is important for us, as a society, to act now. We are sitting ducks. We are waiting for gangs to kill us one by one.

The MSS brought Kenyan boots to Haiti in 2024. However, without a stronger HNP, this is just a Band-Aid solution, which does not begin to address the problem of gangs in Haiti. Our youth are 60% jobless and restless; they need purpose. They do not need handouts.

The Haitian diaspora is strong. Together, they can galvanize at least $4 billion for the motherland. They are deeply involved in the country's affairs. Right now, they need a stake; they do not skepticism. The diaspora can help their homeland with the VPOP initiative, as they did with the Canal project, known as KPK or "Kanal la Pap Kampe."

The VPOP program is Haiti's lifeline. I sent an audio message to friends this week pitching VPOP; they lit up, hope's stirring. Haiti's ready for a spark, and VPOP's it, voluntary, Haitian-led, diaspora-backed. We cannot wait for Port-au-Prince to agree; we can start to protect ourselves with the national police. We can stand up for ourselves. We can stand up for Haiti for the last time.

ACTIVITY SUMMARY

The time has come for the PAPV to emerge as a critical solution for Haiti. This initiative can provide a necessary framework for the revitalization of the Haitian National Police, making it capable of fulfilling its mandate to establish public security across the country. Increasing the number of police officers will be crucial to ensure that law enforcement can effectively counter the threat of gangs. The PAPV can boost the engagement of the diaspora and young people, who are hungry for change and purpose.

This collective dynamic can lead to awareness and immediate action, rather than waiting for uncertain institutional support. With adequate mobilization of Haitian resources and talent, PAPV has the potential to ignite the spark of national renewal. Citizens can stand together to create a safer and more stable environment. It is imperative to act now, as every day lost strengthens the grip of gangs on the country. Therefore, by coming together around the PAPV, Haiti has the opportunity to recover and restore hope. This path may be difficult, but determination and unity will bring tangible results. The time to act is now.

RECOMMENDATIONS AND OUTLINE

Below is a structured outline of the section and the ideas proposed here. This outline is specific to this chapter and only includes the main points and arguments.

Introduction: The Vision" and "Activity Summary"

Outline of Section 3: Why VPOP, Why Now?

- I. Personal Motivation and Mission

A. Professional Journey

- Transition from medicine to law enforcement out of a deeper calling to "heal souls."

- Thirty years of experience in security and policing, with a passion for protecting Haiti

B. Urgency to Act

- Metaphor of Haiti's "dying soul" reflects national collapse and moral crisis

- Personal conviction: the homeland must be saved now, not later

---

- II. Strategic Philosophy: Numerical Superiority

A. Core Doctrine

- Emphasis on "numbers always win" in policing strategy

- Principle of Numerical Superiority (PNS) as part of Police Presence Deployment Strategy (PPDS)

- Goal: Restore police territorial control through overwhelming presence

B. Haiti's Current Deficiency

- HNP is severely understaffed (1.36 officers per 1,000 citizens)

- Stable societies function at ~2.5 officers/1,000; Haiti needs 4–5/1,000 due to extreme gang presence

- Lack of sufficient law enforcement enables gang dominance

C. The VPOP initiative as a Solution

- The VPOP initiative will increase police numbers and reinforce presence
- Makes the HNP "thick" and more operationally effective
- A practical way to reclaim gang zones

- III. Rationale for Immediate Action

A. National Inaction = Vulnerability

- The public is exposed and unprotected; many are "sitting ducks."
- Passive waiting results in growing gang control and civilian casualties

B. Limitations of Foreign Assistance

- MSS (Multinational Security Support) and Kenyan forces offer only a temporary fix
- Without strengthening HNP, foreign presence is a "Band-Aid" solution

C. Untapped National Resources

- 60% of youth unemployment, wasted potential that can be redirected
- Haitian diaspora ($4 billion annually) eager for meaningful engagement, as proven by the KPK canal movement

- The VPOP initiative provides both youth and diaspora with a purpose and path to contribute

D. Grassroots Readiness

- Positive early response to the VPOP idea indicates hope and enthusiasm
- Emphasis on local and immediate action, not waiting for state approval (e.g., Port-au-Prince bureaucracy)

- 3.1 Activity Summary:
- IV. VPOP (PAPV) as a Framework for National Recovery

A. Strengthening HNP Capacity

- Framework to rebuild and professionalize law enforcement
- Critical to establish sustained public security across the country

B. Engagement of Key Stakeholders

- Youth involvement: redirecting energy toward national service and purpose
- Diaspora investment: converting remittances into tangible reform

C. Catalyst for Unity and Action

- Promotes collective awareness and proactive citizenship
- Reduces dependency on dysfunctional institutions

- Offers a path toward rebuilding trust and national stability

D. Call to Urgent Action

- Every day of inaction strengthens gangs

- Unity and determination can overcome obstacles

- The VPOP initiative is positioned as the last chance to reclaim Haiti's future

HOW THE VPOP INITIATIVE WORKS

WHO CAN JOIN THE VPOP INITIATIVE

The VPOP initiative calls on Haiti's 17-35-year-olds, our future, to volunteer. Why them? They are half our population; they are full of fire. They are tired of gangs stealing their lives.

For the VPOP initiative to become a reality, we require 200 individuals to begin. Approximately 50 of them will begin training immediately. The other 150 of the new recruits will report to Cap-Haïtien's commissariats. For this option, there will be no use of force or draft, only a choice. Volunteers will fight for their home. They will protect their neighborhood. As locals, they know the streets, the people, and the stakes. They are not outsiders; they are us.

13

TRAINING: SIX WEEKS TO READINESS

The VPOP plan will be based on the operational tradition of the Haitian national police. We will collaborate with the local police for training. But I will lead the training, which will include intensive session for six weeks; there will be no shortcuts. The training will be built on my Fort Leonard Wood and CAT Team days. Here is the breakdown of what to expect:

WEEKS 1–2: BASICS (VOLUNTEERS WILL LEARN)

Shooting: Sidearms, accuracy, safety, gangs will not wait.

Arrests: Handcuffs, searches, de-escalation, law, not chaos.

During the first two weeks, volunteers will focus on mastering the basics required for effective policing. They will receive training in the safe and accurate use of sidearms to enhance their shooting skills. Such instruction will include best practices for firearm handling and situational awareness, given the urgent risks posed by gangs. The program will also emphasize arrest procedures, teaching volunteers how to use handcuffs effectively and conduct thorough searches. Instruction on de-escalation techniques will ensure that responses prioritize order and the rule of law. These foundational skills will prepare volunteers for the challenges of maintaining security alongside the Haitian National Police.

WEEKS 3–4: TACTICS (VOLUNTEERS WILL LEARN)

Defense: Hold a post, patrol a grid, react to ambushes.

Training: They will learn from my SWAT and CAT Team playbook.

Teamwork: Seven teams, 28–30 each.

Foundational skills: They will learn to move as one.

During weeks three and four, volunteers will focus on tactical training designed to enhance operational effectiveness and security. Defensive skills will be emphasized, including how to hold a post, patrol assigned areas, and respond effectively to ambush scenarios. The curriculum will draw insights from proven strategies and techniques found in SWAT and Counter-Assault Team (CAT) playbooks. Teamwork will also be a cornerstone of this phase. Volunteers will be organized into seven teams, each comprising 28 to 30 individuals. Training will ensure members learn to coordinate and move as a unified force. These efforts may improve situational readiness and cohesion in joint operations with the Haitian National Police.

WEEKS 5–6: COMMUNITY POLICING (VOLUNTEERS WILL LEARN)

Trust: Talk to elders, kids, vendors.

Training: They will learn to win hearts, not just fights.

Intel: Spot gang moves; report clean.

Foundational kills: They will become the eyes for the HNP.

Weeks 5–6 of the Voluntary Police Officer Program will focus on the principles of community policing. Volunteers will learn how to build trust within the neighborhoods they serve. They will interact with elders, children, and local vendors to foster mutual respect. Their training will emphasize winning the trust and cooperation of the people rather than relying solely on force.

Volunteers will also develop skills in intelligence gathering. They will be trained to observe gang activities and movements without interfering directly. Accurate and timely reporting to the Haitian National Police (HNP) will become one of their core responsibilities. These efforts will help strengthen partnerships between the HNP and local communities. Volunteers can play a key role in bridging the gap between law enforcement and civilians. Community policing may enhance security and provide a foundation for long-term stability in Haiti.

Fifty trainees per class, two cycles (100 in total), then a third (100 more). We will use Cap-Haïtien's two stations, one is MINUSTAH-built, solid. Gear's basic: pistols, vests, radios, nothing fancy, just functional.

Each training class will include fifty trainees, with two cycles initially planned to train a total of one hundred participants. A third training cycle may also be conducted to double the total number of trainees to two hundred. Training operations will utilize the two police stations in Cap-Haïtien, including one constructed by MINUSTAH, which is designed to meet modern safety and operational standards. Equipment issued to trainees will remain practical and effective, including basic items such as pistols, protective vests, and communication radios. The program will prioritize functionality over sophistication to ensure ease of use and reliability in the field.

DEPLOYMENT: SIX MONTHS, ONE CITY

Starting July 2025 (tentative date), 200 VPOP volunteers will join 100 HNP officers in Cap-Haïtien, 450,000 people, moderate crime (60 incidents/month), a winnable fight. We will cover 15 km^2, urban core first, which will be split into seven grids:

Clear: Patrols push gangs out, 3:1 odds (200 vs. ~50–70 gang fighters, per 2024 MSS estimates).

Hold: Posts at key spots (RN1, port, markets); will maintain 24/7 presence.

Build: Foot patrols, community talks, show we are here to stay.

Patrol operations may help to push gang elements out of critical areas and restore a sense of security. The initiative will create an advantage by ensuring a consistent and overwhelming presence. It will deploy more personnel than gang forces to maximize control and stability. Estimates from the 2024 MSS mission suggest a ratio of three officers to every gang combatant. Effective coordination during patrols will help leverage this numerical superiority against groups of approximately 50 to 70 gang members.

The program will establish posts at critical locations, including RN1, the port, and major markets. Officers can maintain a consistent and visible 24/7 presence at these sites. These strategic placements may help deter criminal activity and enhance public safety. The deployment of personnel at these key areas will strengthen security coordination with the Haitian National Police. This approach can provide a reliable framework for monitoring and responding to potential threats.

The program will establish regular foot patrols to increase police presence and strengthen community trust. Officers may engage directly with citizens to foster open communication and collaboration. Organizing community talks will help address local concerns and reinforce public confidence in security efforts.

These initiatives can create a sense of stability and demonstrate a long-term commitment to public safety. Establishing visibility and maintaining consistent interaction with residents will encourage cooperation between citizens and law enforcement. Such efforts will lay the foundation for sustainable security improvements in partnership with the Haitian National Police.

Seven fast vehicles (one per team) and one armored unit (MSS loan) keep us mobile. Drones, two per team, spot gang moves. We are not invading Port-au-Prince; we are proving the VPOP initiative works where it can.

Seven fast vehicles, allocated as one per team, will enhance mobility and rapid response capabilities. An additional armored unit, provided through an MSS loan, may offer reinforced protection during critical operations. Each team can deploy two drones to monitor gang movements from above. These tools will contribute to a more effective and coordinated effort in supporting the Haitian National Police.

THE GOAL

The VPOP initiative may achieve three critical objectives within a nine-month cycle, divided into six weeks of recurring, but also intensive, training, two weeks of being tested on the field, and seven months of full active police patrols. The program will enhance the operational capacity of the Haitian National Police by incorporating well-trained volunteers into their ranks. It can help establish a more visible and effective community presence to deter crime and foster trust among local citizens.

The VPOP initiative may also improve the collective security environment by deploying prepared individuals who understand the unique challenges of Haiti's safety landscape. This structured approach to training and patrolling will ensure a positive impact on public safety. This strategy will help strengthen collaborative efforts for crime prevention across the nation.

In nine months, six weeks training, two weeks of probation period, and seven months of intensive patrolling, we should hit three marks:

Crime Down 20%: From 60 incidents/month to 48, which will be tracked by HNP logs.

Trust Up 70%: Surveys say "yes" to "Do you feel safer?" Let us let the locals decide.

Gangs Retreat: 15 km^2 with our plan. There will be no gang flags flying.

Gauging success: The MSS will confirm our exploit.

The VPOP initiative has the potential to reduce crime rates in Haiti significantly. Data from the Haitian National Police (HNP) logs indicate a 20% decrease in criminal activity, dropping from 60 reported incidents per month to 48. This decline demonstrates the program's capacity to enhance public safety and support law enforcement efforts. Such a measurable impact highlights how community-based initiatives can complement and strengthen the operations of the HNP. Expanding the reach of the VPOP initiative could amplify these positive outcomes and will further safeguard communities in Haiti.

Trust in the VPOP initiative may increase community confidence in public safety. Surveys indicate that approximately 70% of respondents feel safer due to the program. The initiative gives locals a voice in evaluating its effectiveness. When asked directly, many residents confirm an improved sense of security. This feedback would suggest that the program can strengthen trust between the community and law enforcement. Collaborative efforts with the Haitian National Police may further enhance this perception. The data will underscore the potential for The VPOP initiative to make a meaningful impact on safety in Haiti.

If gang members were to retreat, it would lead to the reclamation of a 15 km^2 area, eventually falling under secure control. No gang flags would be visible within this territory, potentially signaling progress in restoring order. The MSS could confirm the strategic advance and stabilization of this zone. Such an achievement might contribute to broader efforts aimed at rebuilding security and governance in the region.

If it works, we scale, Jacmel, Léogâne, beyond. If it falters, we fix it. No bluffing just results.

If the program proves successful, it will expand to areas such as Jacmel, Léogâne, and beyond. We will adjust strategies to address any challenges that arise. This initiative focuses on measurable outcomes rather than sweeping promises. Every effort will prioritize tangible improvements over rhetoric.

ACTIVITY SUMMARY

The VPOP initiative represents a transformative approach to strengthen the security landscape in Haiti. By engaging the country's youth in active volunteer roles, we are creating a model for community empowerment and resilience. The emphasis on training, collaboration, and community trust forms the bedrock of this program.

The structured training over six weeks will equip volunteers with essential skills necessary for effective policing. The focus on community policing will help build bridges between law enforcement and civilians. It will foster trust, which can significantly enhance public safety. Through direct engagement with the community, volunteers will become advocates for change rather than enforcers, working to restore confidence among residents.

As the initiative unfolds, achieving measurable goals will be paramount. A targeted reduction in crime rates by 20% can signal the beginning of a safer environment. Improved public perception, reflected by a 70% increase in community trust, will indicate progress in collaborative security efforts. Reclaiming a substantial area from gang control will further solidify gains made and demonstrate the effectiveness of local involvement.

By utilizing resources like fast vehicles and drones, operational efficiency will increase. These tools will provide critical support in maintaining order and enhancing patrol capabilities. The partnership with the Haitian National Police strengthens the foundation of this initiative, ensuring seamless cooperation between trained volunteers and professionals.

The overarching objective is clear: to create a sustainable security framework in which communities not only feel safe but also take part in upholding that safety. The VPOP initiative can serve as a replicable model across different regions. If challenges emerge, they will be addressed with adaptability and dedication.

This initiative can lay the groundwork for a safer, more secure Haiti. It will help restore hope and stability for future generations. If successful, the plan will not just be a security restoration program; it will be a movement toward empowerment, resilience, and community-led safety.

RECOMMENDATIONS AND OUTLINE

Below is a structured outline of the section and the ideas proposed here. This outline is specific to this chapter and only includes the main points and arguments.

Outline of Section 4: How the VPOP initiative Works

- 4.1 Who Can Join the VPOP Initiative
  - Target Group: Haitian youth aged 17–35
  - Half of the nation's population, full of energy and urgency
  - Motivated to reclaim their communities from gangs
  - Enrollment Plan:

- First 50 volunteers immediately, then 150 more
- No draft; entirely voluntary
- Local Advantage:
- Volunteers come from the neighborhoods they serve
- They understand the culture, terrain, and people
- They are defending their own homes

- 4.2 Training: Six Weeks to Readiness
- Overview:
  - Led by the program founder with experience from Fort Leonard Wood and CAT Team
  - In partnership with Haitian National Police
  - Emphasizes readiness, discipline, and purpose
- 4.2.1 Weeks 1–2: Basics
  - Shooting: Safe handling, sidearm accuracy, immediate readiness for gang threats
  - Arrests: Cuffing, searching, de-escalation, focus on rule of law
- 4.2.2 Weeks 3–4: Tactics

- Defense: Holding posts, patrolling zones, reacting to ambushes (SWAT/CAT methods)
- Teamwork: Seven teams of 28–30 trainees; learn coordination and unit movement
- 4.2.3 Weeks 5–6: Community Policing
- Trust-building: Dialogue with locals, elders, children, merchants
- Intelligence: Observing gang behavior, reporting cleanly to HNP
- Training Logistics:
  - 50 trainees per cycle, initially two cycles (total 100), with a third planned (total 200)
  - The use of two Cap-Haïtien police stations, including a MINUSTAH-built one
  - Equipment: sidearms, vests, radios, functional, not flashy

---

- 4.3 Deployment: Six Months, One City
- Launch Timeline and Location:
  - Start date: July 2025 (tentative)
  - Deployment in Cap-Haïtien (450,000 population)
  - Selected for manageable crime levels (60 incidents/month)

- Deployment Strategy: "Clear, Hold, Build"
- Clear: Push gangs out of urban core using 3:1 advantage (200 VPOP + 100 HNP vs. 50–70 gang fighters)
- Hold: Establish 24/7 presence at strategic locations (RN1, port, markets)
- Build: Foot patrols and community engagement to demonstrate long-term commitment
- Support Tools:
  - 7 fast vehicles (1 per team)
  - 1 armored vehicle (loaned by MSS)
  - 2 drones per team for aerial surveillance
  - Not targeting Port-au-Prince, proving the model works in Cap-Haïtien first

---

4.4 The Goal

- Nine-Month Mission Breakdown:
  - 6 weeks training
  - 2 weeks of field testing
  - 7 months of active deployment
- Three Core Objectives:
1. Crime Reduction:
   - 20% drop in incidents (from 60 to 48/month per HNP data)
2. Community Trust:
   - 70% of residents say they feel safer (survey-based metric)
3. Territorial Control:
   - 15 km^2 reclaimed from gangs, no gang flags, MSS verification
4. Scalability:
   - If successful, expand to Jacmel, Léogâne, and beyond
   - If challenges arise, adapt and improve
   - Commitment to results over promises

4.5 Activity Summary

- Youth Empowerment:
  - Harnesses untapped energy and readiness of Haitian youth
- Community Trust:
  - Will prioritize relationship-building with residents
- Operational Strength:

- o Combines rigorous training with practical field deployment

- Security Gains:
  - o Goals of reduced crime, increased safety perception, and reclaimed territory

- Scalable Model:
  - o The VPOP initiative as a replicable framework for national security transformation

- Partnerships:
  - o Strong coordination with Haitian National Police and diaspora support

- Long-term Vision:
  - o A grassroots movement for national renewal and citizen-led protection

The Voluntary Police Officer Program (VPOP)

THE DIASPORA'S ROLE

WHY THE DIASPORA?

Our diaspora, 3 million in the U.S., Canada, France, holds Haiti's lifeline: $4 billion yearly, 40% of our GDP. You have watched us suffer, 2010 quake, 2021 assassination, 2024 gang surge. You have sent money, prayed, and waited (for a better Haiti, which never came). The VPOP initiative is your chance to fight back.

Haiti's diaspora represents a vital lifeline for the nation. They contribute approximately $4 billion annually, which makes up 40% of the country's GDP. Members of the diaspora have witnessed Haiti's challenges firsthand, from the devastating earthquake in 2010 to the political instability following the 2021 assassination of President Jovenel Moïse and the escalating gang violence in 2024.

After the 2010 earthquake, many Haitian diaspora members provided financial support to Haiti; they offered prayers; they hoped for meaningful change, yet transformative progress has remained elusive. The VPOP initiative offers a concrete opportunity for the diaspora to take active steps towards improving security and stability in Haiti. This initiative can empower individuals to directly contribute to the fight against violence and help build a safer and more unified future.

WHY ME?

I have lived among you, studied at your university, trained in Missouri, I know your heart and your power. This is not charity; it is ownership.

I have lived within your communities abroad; I understand your struggles, aspirations, and your dreams to return home someday. I, too, share the same dreams. But I am in the position to make a tangible difference to help restore peace and security in the homeland.

I have an extensive background in various fields of study. My education at the UNE (Mexico), John Jay College of Criminal Justice, Villanova, Widener Law, and North Carolina Central, among others (academic institutions attended), constitutes a tremendous asset to my understanding of the need for safety and security in Haiti. My academic background and experience, coupled with my training in Missouri, DSS (Mobile Division), CIMO, SWAT (CI), Anti-Riot (MO), and USP (Presidential Security Unit), have equipped me with knowledge to contribute effectively to the VPOP plan. My personal and professional backgrounds constitute an important asset. I will dedicate myself to this plan wholeheartedly. This initiative will not rely on charity but on the need to foster a collective sense of ownership and responsibility for Haiti's future, which must begin with law, order, peace, and security.

WHAT WE NEED: $1 MILLION

The VPOP initiative will operate with an efficient budget, allocating $1 million for the pilot program in Cap-Haïtien. Every dollar invested will directly fund on-the-ground activities to improve security and support operations. This lean financial approach may maximize impact and ensure that resources are used effectively.

The program's streamlined funding will allow for targeted interventions that complement the efforts of the Haitian National Police (HNP). This allocation strategy can strengthen collaboration and focus on tangible security improvements within the community.

The VPOP's initial approach, $1M for Cap-Haïtien's pilot program, every dollar on the ground:

Training ($200,000): Six weeks, 200 volunteers, $100K per cycle. Ranges, ammo, my time, covered.

Stipends ($360,000): $200/month per volunteer, 6 months, keeps them fed, committed.

Gear ($140,000): Pistols, vests, radios, drones, $700/volunteer, basics only.

Vehicles ($200,000): Seven patrol cars ($175K), one armored ($25K via MSS).

Stations ($100,000): Upgrade Cap-Haïtien's two posts, roof, power, desks.

The Voluntary Police Officer Program will provide intensive training for Haitian participants to strengthen security efforts. Each training cycle will last six weeks and will accommodate 200 volunteers. The program will allocate $100,000 per cycle to cover essential costs. Training will include the use of shooting ranges, ammunition, and specialized instruction. These resources will enhance the skills and operational readiness of volunteers to support the Haitian National Police. A total of $200,000 will fund this critical capacity-building initiative.

The program will allocate $360,000 in stipends to support volunteers participating in the initiative. Each volunteer may receive $200 per month for a period of six months. These stipends can help ensure that participants have access to basic necessities, such as food and other essential resources. Providing financial support can also encourage greater commitment to the program's objectives. This approach may promote both stability and sustained engagement among volunteers, which will enhance the program's overall effectiveness.

The program will allocate $200,000 toward acquiring essential vehicles to strengthen patrol and operational capabilities. Seven standard patrol cars will be purchased at a total cost of $175,000. Additionally, $25,000 will be invested in procuring one armored vehicle through MSS. These vehicles will enhance mobility, expand coverage, and improve the responsiveness of the Haitian National

Police. The inclusion of an armored vehicle may also provide added protection in high-risk areas, ensuring officer safety during critical operations.

The program will focus on upgrading two police stations in Cap-Haïtien to enhance their infrastructure and functionality. Each station will receive necessary improvements, such as installing durable roofing to ensure safety during adverse weather conditions. Reliable power systems will be implemented to support uninterrupted operations and communications. Officers will benefit from new desks that can help optimize their workspace and efficiency. These upgrades may improve the overall capacity of the stations to serve the community and support the Haitian National Police in maintaining security.

No fat, $5,000 per volunteer, total. Compared to MSS's $600M budget, VPOP's a bargain that works.

The VPOP initiative may offer a cost-effective solution to improving security in Haiti. Each volunteer will require a funding allocation of $5,000 in total. This financial structure stands in stark contrast to the $600 million budget for the MSS initiative of the Haitian National Police.

POP can present a valuable alternative that maximizes impact while minimizing costs. Its streamlined approach will help address critical security needs while optimizing resource allocation. Implementing this program may enhance safety and foster stability across local communities in a sustainable and affordable manner.

HOW TO FUND THE VPOP

The VPOP initiative could be funded through two primary avenues. The first option may involve direct contributions from international donors, including governments, nonprofit organizations, or private entities interested in supporting Haiti's security infrastructure. This type of funding can help ensure that essential resources, training programs, and operational expenses are covered effectively.

Another possibility for financing could come from collaborative partnerships within Haiti, such as local businesses, civic groups, and community organizations. These partnerships might help create a sustainable funding model by promoting shared accountability and local ownership of the program. By diversifying funding sources, The VPOP initiative could improve its resilience and operational reach, which will help fostering greater cooperation with

Two ways are worthy of note here:

the Haitian National Police and strengthening security efforts nationwide.

Crowdfunding: "VPOP Haiti" online, $100 gets a "Haiti's Hero" badge, $500 names a patrol team.

Goal: $500K from 5,000 donors. It starts small, grows fast.

VPOP Bonds: $1,000 each, 3% return in 5 years, $500K from 500 big players (doctors, pastors, business folk). Haiti will repay via future taxes or donor grants.

The VPOP initiative in Haiti aims to incorporate innovative crowdfunding methods to enhance security in collaboration with the Haitian National Police. An online platform titled "VPOP Haiti" will serve as a centralized space for donations and public engagement. A contribution of $100 can reward donors with a "Haiti's Hero" badge, recognizing their commitment to the initiative.

Donors contributing $500 may have the opportunity to name a local patrol team, adding a personal connection to the program's outcomes. The campaign aspires to raise $500,000 by engaging 5,000 donors, emphasizing collective effort and community support. Initial efforts will begin on a modest scale but have the potential to expand rapidly as participation grows. By blending technology with civic engagement, crowdfunding can stimulate both financial support and public trust in this essential security program.

The VPOP initiative will finance its operations through the sale of bonds valued at $1,000 each. These bonds will offer investors a 3% return over a five-year period. The program seeks to raise $500,000 by engaging 500 key stakeholders, including doctors, pastors, and business leaders. Haiti may repay these bonds using future tax revenues or financial support from international donor grants. This approach can attract influential community members to invest in national security while fostering long-term financial sustainability.

Mix both, $500K crowd funding, $500K bonds. You choose how much, when.

The VPOP initiative will strengthen security efforts in Haiti in partnership with the Haitian National Police. The initiative will aim to recruit civilian volunteers who can assist in safeguarding communities. These volunteers may receive basic training on law enforcement practices and community engagement.

The program could improve coordination between civilians and law enforcement to address localized security concerns. Funding options may include a blend of $500,000 from crowd-sourced contributions and $500,000 in bonds. This dual approach will offer flexibility in resource allocation based on immediate needs. The amounts allotted and the best times to distribute funds are up to the program designers. By enhancing security systems and integrating civilian support, The VPOP initiative will provide a safer environment and promote stability across Haiti.

ACCOUNTABILITY

The VPOP initiative can strengthen security in Haiti by complementing the efforts of the Haitian National Police. It will provide structured support and expand the capacity of law enforcement to address local challenges. Participants will receive training to ensure they uphold professional standards and community trust. Regular evaluations may help maintain accountability and improve overall performance. This partnership between volunteers and police forces can enhance public safety and stability.

Your money's safe:

Diaspora Board: Five reps, U.S., Canada, France, audit via Zoom. You pick 'em.

My reports will include Monthly videos, training clips, patrol walks, volunteer faces (with consent). See your dollars at work live.

HNP/MSS Oversight: Joint logs track crime, trust, datum is open, no cooking books.

The safety and accountability of funds will remain a top priority under the VPOP. A Diaspora Board with five representatives from the United States, Canada, and France will oversee financial audits. These representatives may be selected by members of the Haitian diaspora, ensuring transparency and trust in the process. Audits will be conducted remotely via Zoom, allowing for efficient oversight regardless of geographical location. This approach can help build confidence among contributors and stakeholders.

The VPOP initiative will provide monthly reports to enhance transparency and accountability. These reports will consist of short video updates highlighting essential training sessions designed to prepare volunteers for their duties. Captured patrol walks will offer a direct view into day-to-day security operations, providing valuable insights into the program's on-the-ground impact.

Volunteer faces, shared with their consent, may highlight the individuals contributing to Haiti's safety and security. Supporters can watch their contributions take effect through these dynamic visual updates. This reporting approach will help further connect donors to the program's tangible outcomes.

The Haitian National Police (HNP) and the Ministry of Public Security (MSS) will oversee joint logs to ensure accurate tracking of criminal activity and public trust metrics. These logs can provide a centralized and transparent record-keeping system to monitor progress and identify areas for improvement. Direct access to this data should promote accountability and discourage any manipulation of reports or records. This framework may enhance trust between law enforcement agencies and the communities they serve. Reliable data collection will also support informed decision-making and policy adjustments in response to emerging challenges.

If we hit 20% crime drop, 70% trust, 15 km^2 secure, you will know it worked. If not, I will tell you why and fix it.

The VPOP initiative will aim to achieve measurable results in Haiti by collaborating closely with the Haitian National Police. A crime reduction of 20% will demonstrate the program's success in enhancing safety and deterring criminal activity. Public trust levels reaching 70% will signify strengthened relationships between law enforcement and communities.

Securing an area of 15 square kilometers will reflect tangible progress in stabilizing local territories. If we fail to meet these benchmarks, we will thoroughly evaluate the program to identify its shortcomings. Appropriate adjustments will ensure the initiative fulfills its purpose effectively.

ACTIVITY SUMMARY

The role of the Haitian diaspora is pivotal to the future of Haiti. With substantial financial contributions that account for 40% of the national GDP, diaspora members possess the power to instigate genuine change. The VPOP initiative represents a transformative opportunity for the diaspora to participate actively in reshaping Haiti's security landscape. By investing directly in training and local engagement, The VPOP initiative enables volunteers to foster a sense of agency and responsibility toward their homeland.

The $1 million budget for the pilot program illustrates a strategic allocation that prioritizes efficiency and targeted impact. By focusing on essential resources, training, stipends, gear, vehicles, and infrastructure improvements, this program can effectively enhance the operational capabilities of the Haitian National Police and empower local communities.

Innovative funding approaches such as crowdfunding and bond issuance may diversify support while fostering local ownership. These mechanisms can create a sustainable financial foundation and galvanize collective efforts in the diaspora. Increased volunteer engagement will not only bolster security but also build trust and cooperation between community members and law enforcement agencies.

Accountability and transparency will remain central to VPOP's mission. The establishment of a Diaspora Board for financial oversight and regular reporting will ensure that contributors can observe the direct outcomes of their investments.

By tracking crime rates, community trust levels, and operational advancements, participants and supporters will be equipped to understand the program's effectiveness.

If successful, the VPOP initiative will not only improve safety but also lay the groundwork for a more cohesive and resilient Haiti. As we look ahead, this initiative can unify the diaspora and local stakeholders in a shared vision of progress. Together, they can help address the urgent needs facing Haiti and foster lasting stability for future generations. Your involvement can turn hope into reality.

RECOMMENDATIONS AND OUTLINE

Below is a structured outline of the section and the ideas proposed here. This outline is specific to this chapter and only includes the main points and arguments.

Introduction: The Vision" and "Activity Summary"

The Diaspora's Role (Outline)

- 5.1 Why the Diaspora?
- Scale of Support
- Over 3 million Haitians live abroad (U.S., Canada, France)
- Contribute ~$4 billion annually (40% of Haiti's GDP)
- Shared History of Crisis Response
- 2010 earthquake
- 2021 assassination of President Moïse
- 2024 gang violence surge
- The VPOP initiative as a Turning Point
- Offers diaspora a direct role in Haiti's security
- Transitions support from passive (remittances, prayers) to active (community protection)
- A move from hope to tangible, strategic action

- 5.2 Why Me?
- Personal Connection
    - Lived in diaspora communities, studied and trained in the U.S
    - Understands the diaspora's frustrations and aspirations

- Relevant Training & Expertise
    - Academic institutions: UNE (Mexico), John Jay, Villanova, Widener, NCCU
    - Security training: DSS (Mobile Division), CIMO, SWAT, Anti-Riot, USP (Presidential Security Unit)
- Leadership Commitment
    - Prepared to fully commit to implementing VPOP
    - Emphasizes ownership, not charity, diaspora-led security and reform

---

- 5.3 What We Need: $1 Million (Pilot in Cap-Haïtien)
- Total Budget: $1,000,000, fully allocated to ground-level operations
- Line-Item Breakdown:
- Training ($200,000)
    - 2 cycles, 6 weeks each, 200 volunteers total
    - Covers facilities, ranges, ammo, instruction
- Stipends ($360,000)
    - $200/month × 200 volunteers × 6 months

- Supports basic needs, encourages sustained engagement
- Gear ($140,000)
    - Basics only: vests, pistols, radios, drones
    - $700 per volunteer
- Vehicles ($200,000)
    - 7 patrol cars ($175K), 1 armored vehicle via MSS ($25K)
- Infrastructure ($100,000)
    - Renovate 2 Cap-Haïtien stations: roofing, power, desks
- Cost Comparison:
- VPOP = $5,000 per volunteer
- MSS = $600 million annual security budget
- The VPOP initiative is a lean, high impact alternative

- 5.4 How to Fund the VPOP
- A. Crowdfunding
- Platform: "VPOP Haiti"
- Goal: $500,000 from 5,000 donors
    - $100 = "Haiti's Hero" badge

- $500 = Name a patrol team
- Emphasizes small-donor engagement, rapid scalability
- B. VPOP Bonds
- Goal: $500,000 from 500 investors
    - $1,000 bond per investor
    - 3% return over 5 years
- Target: diaspora professionals (e.g., doctors, pastors, business leaders)
- Repayment via future taxes or donor grants
- C. Hybrid Model
- Combines crowdfunding + bond sales
- Flexible and scalable funding mix based on timing and donor type

---

- 5.5 Accountability
- A. Financial Oversight
- Diaspora Oversight Board
    - 5 members: U.S., Canada, France
    - Selected by diaspora; audit via Zoom
- B. Transparency & Reporting

- Monthly Updates
  - Short videos: training sessions, patrols, volunteer interviews (with consent)
  - Real-time connection to impact
- Joint Logs with HNP/MSS
  - Tracks crime stats, patrols, and trust metrics
  - Open, tamper-proof records
- C. Performance Metrics
  - Benchmarks:
    - 20% crime reduction
    - 70% public trust
    - 15 km^2 secured
  - Evaluation & Adjustment:
    - If targets are missed, full accountability and responsive corrections will follow

---

- 5.6 Activity Summary
  - Strategic Diaspora Role
    - Financial engine behind 40% of GDP

  - Now positioned to drive security reform and national restoration
- Efficient, Focused Investment
  - $1M covers training, stipends, gear, vehicles, and infrastructure
  - Low-cost, high-yield model
- Innovative Funding
  - Dual model: crowdfunding + bond sales
  - Builds public ownership and long-term sustainability
- Institutional Accountability
  - Diaspora Board
  - Monthly video reports
  - Transparent data logs with HNP/MSS
- Measurable Outcomes
  - Safer communities
  - Stronger police-community relations
  - Model for scalable national security reform
- Unified Call to Action

- The VPOP initiative is your opportunity to directly shape Haiti's future

- Join as a supporter, investor, and stakeholder in a peaceful, unified nation

WHY THE VPOP INITIATIVE WINS

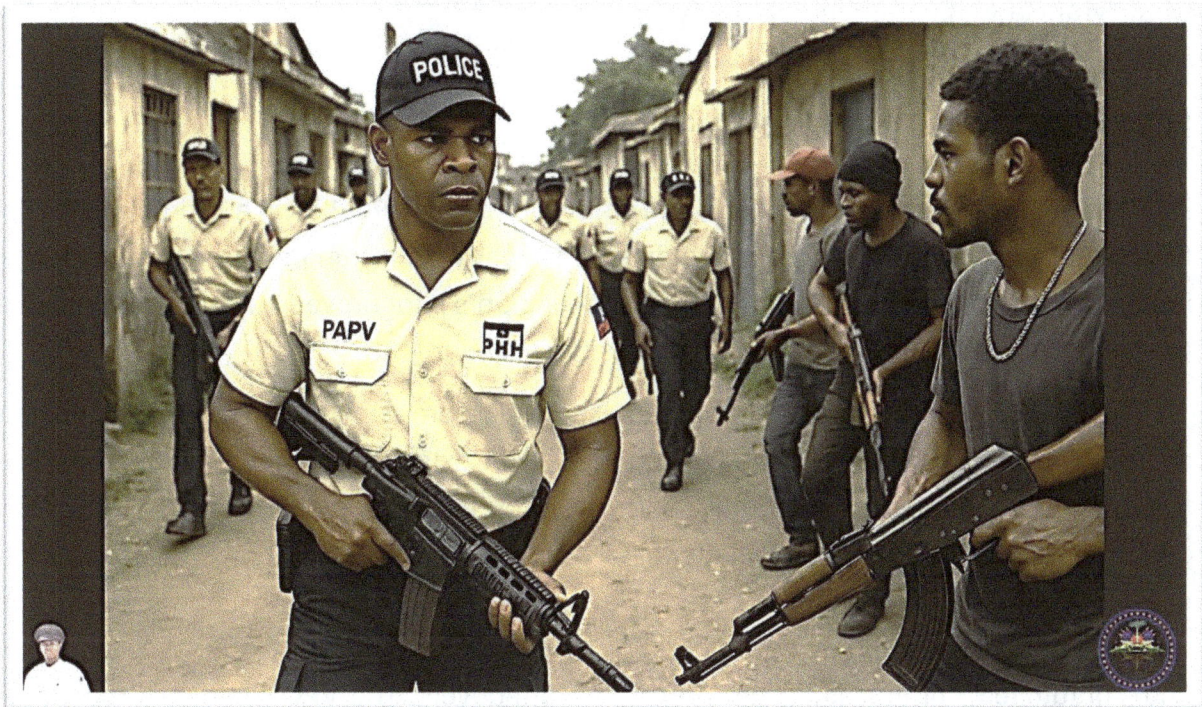

NUMBERS BEAT GANGS

The PNS is not just a theory; it is a fact. Gangs rule where police are weak. Therefore, deploying 200 VPOP and 100 HNP officers in Cap-Haïtien can change the situation considerably. Three-to-one odds (300 vs. 50–70 gang fighters) mean that the police do not just chase gangs; we control them; we restrict them affectively. My CAT Team days have taught me how to overwhelm terrorists and not try to outsmart them when it is not necessary. The VPOP initiative is the muscle that the Haitian national police have missed.

The principle of strength in numbers could significantly undermine the dominance of gangs in Haiti. Gangs thrive in areas where law enforcement remains undermanned and ineffective. Deploying 200 Voluntary Police Officers (VPOP) alongside 100 Haitian National Police

(HNP) in key regions, such as Cap-Haïtien, may shift the power dynamic.

A combined force of 300 officers could easily counter the estimated 50 to 70 gang members typically controlling these areas. This three-to-one numerical advantage would grant law enforcement the ability not only to disrupt gang activities but also to establish lasting control. Experience from tactical units emphasizes the importance of overwhelming force over strategic nuance when dealing with such threats. The VPOP initiative could provide the strength and manpower that Haiti has long lacked to restore peace and security.

HOPE BREAKS PARALYSIS

Haitians are tired of gangs, blackouts, and empty promises. VPOP's not a decree or a foreign fix; it is us, youth volunteering, and the diaspora is paying. My friends heard my audio, they felt it. One friend said, "This could work." Cap-Haïtien's pilot proves it works; next, we plan to scale the project. Hope's a weapon, gangs cannot shoot that.

The VPOP initiative aims to strengthen security in Haiti by supporting the Haitian National Police through a collaborative and community-driven approach. Haitians are eager to overcome the challenges posed by widespread gang activity, power outages, and unfulfilled promises. The VPOP initiative will rely on local youth volunteers and financial support from the Haitian diaspora to create actionable change.

The program is not a top-down mandate or an external solution; it is a grassroots effort led by those committed to rebuilding their communities. Early feedback from pilot initiatives in Cap-Haïtien will indicate strong potential for success. If scaled effectively, The VPOP initiative may serve as a transformative model for restoring hope and resilience, both of which are intangible forces that can undermine criminal influence and strengthen collective resolve.

DIASPORA MAKES IT REAL

Haiti's budget [is broke] does not have money, $100M for security, half swallowed by VIPs. The diaspora's $4B is a major card; it is our ace. MSS and the UN talk big, $1M from the VPOP initiative will help us start small and win fast. The diaspora can fund 200 volunteers; we can reclaim 15 km². Next year, we aim to reach 1,000 volunteers and reclaim 50km.

The Haitian government currently faces significant financial constraints. They are allocating a measly amount of money, which many estimate as less than

$100 million, to national security efforts, with a substantial portion of that money being diverted to VIP-related expenditures. While there is funding allocated to intelligence gathering or other related operations, that money is not spent in a transparent manner, which leads many observers to doubt whether it is spent for its intended purposes.

Despite these challenges, the Haitian diaspora represents a major resource with an annual contribution of $4 billion to the national economy, providing an opportunity to strengthen security in the country. A modest initial investment of $1 million from the diaspora could launch the VPOP, which may immediately deploy 200 trained volunteers to collaborate with the Haitian National Police. This effort will potentially help reclaim and secure an estimated 15 square kilometers of territory. Scaling the initiative further could lead to the mobilization of 1,000 volunteers, expanding coverage to 50 square kilometers within the following year. The involvement of the diaspora could transform security efforts into tangible, impactful outcomes.

THE VPOP INITIATIVE IS OURS

There are no white saviors or council delays, The VPOP initiative is fully a Haitian initiative. I have trained police officers, led teams, and studied this, I am not guessing; this is a fact. The second cohort of CAT Team members are my brainchild, as I helped train these individuals with the collaboration of others. I have done this before; I can do it again. See the image below.

The Voluntary Police Officer Program (VPOP)

You, in the diaspora, have done your part. You have kept Haiti alive with remittances; now we fight together. Gangs will lose when we unite.

The VPOP initiative can offer a tangible solution to improving security in Haiti. It will collaborate with the Haitian National Police to strengthen law enforcement efforts. The program is rooted in Haitian communities and designed to address local realities. Its framework incorporates expertise in training officers, leading teams, and studying policing methods tailored to Haiti's unique challenges.

Haitian diaspora members have sustained the country through remittances, and their support will remain vital for collaborative initiatives. A unified front between citizens, law enforcement, and the international community has the potential to weaken gang influence and restore order. The VPOP initiative will focus on mobilizing local resources, fostering solidarity, and empowering Haitian leadership to tackle security issues.

The strategy is not abstract or experimental; it draws from proven approaches and collective commitment. Ending gang violence may become achievable when shared determination translates into coordinated action. See the image below.

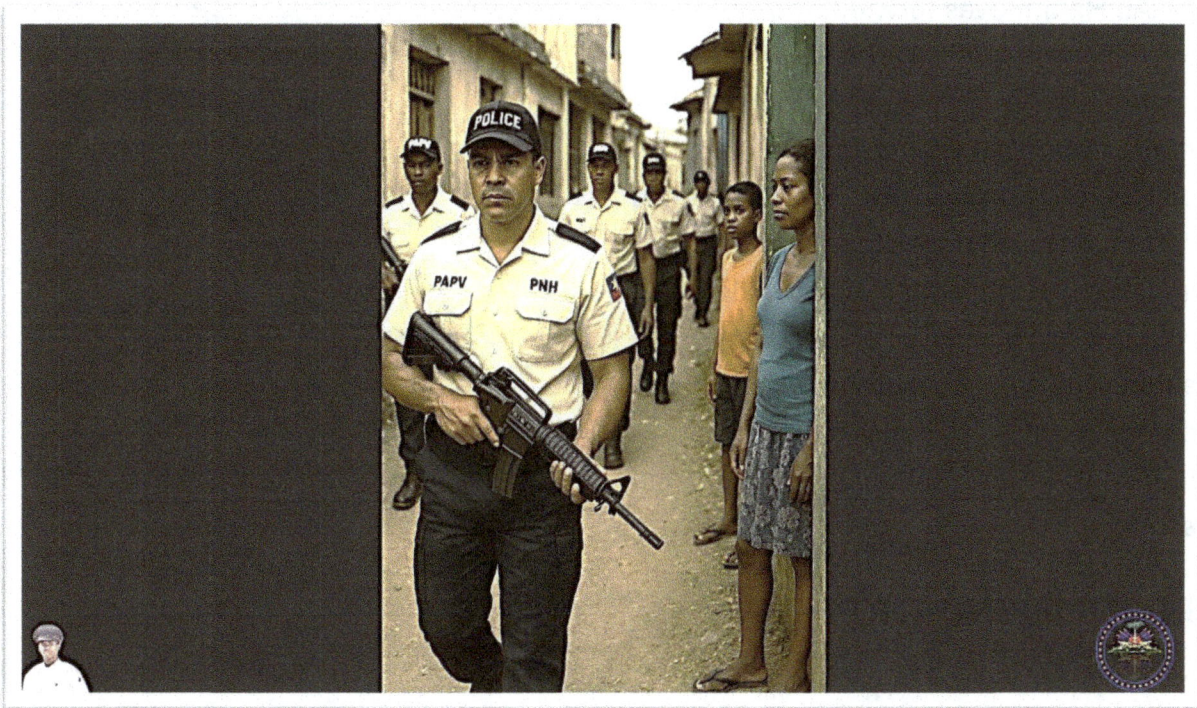

ACTIVITY SUMMARY

The VPOP initiative represents a decisive step toward reclaiming Haiti from the grip of gang violence. By mobilizing local youth and engaging with the diaspora, it will harness the power of community-driven action. The projected deployment of 200 VPOP volunteers existing alongside the HNP can significantly alter the security landscape, fostering a sense of confidence that has long been absent. A sustained effort can embed these positive changes into the fabric of society.

The engagement of the diaspora is critical. Their financial contributions have the potential to elevate grassroots efforts from mere concepts to actionable strategies. With a $1 million initial investment, the possibility of rapidly reclaiming key territories emerges, which will help leading to a safer environment for all Haitians. Scaling the initiative to involve 1,000 volunteers can further solidify this renewed sense of hope and security.

Importantly, this initiative prioritizes local leadership and expertise. It will not depend on external intervention or theoretical solutions. Instead, the VPOP initiative will draw on the strengths of the Haitian people, reinforcing their resolve and commitment to a brighter future. The combined forces of local volunteers and the Haitian National Police create a formidable approach to combating organized crime.

As Haiti moves forward, the necessity for unity and collective action cannot be overstated. Nevertheless, the potential for transformational change lies within this collaborative framework. A strengthened community effort will diminish gang influence, restore vital public order, and which will help pave the way toward a safer, more prosperous Haiti. The commitment to this vision can create a foundation for enduring peace and security.

RECOMMENDATIONS AND OUTLINE

Below is a structured outline of the section and the ideas proposed here. This outline is specific to this chapter and only includes the main points and arguments.

Introduction: The Vision" and "Activity Summary"

Why The VPOP initiative Wins (Outline)

- 6.1 Numbers Beat Gangs
  - Principle: Power in Numbers
    - Gangs dominate where security is weak and outnumbered
    - PNS (Patrol, Neutralize, Stabilize) is not a theory, it is a proven strategy
  - Tactical Deployment
    - 200 VPOP + 100 HNP = 300 officers vs. 50–70 gang fighters in Cap-Haïtien
    - 3:1 ratio overwhelms gangs; shifts from reactive to proactive control
- Operational Insight
  - Experience from CAT Team confirms: force beats finesse in asymmetrical urban threats
  - The VPOP initiative provides the muscle Haiti has long lacked

---

- 6.2 Hope Breaks Paralysis
- Emotional Shift
  - Public frustration: gangs, blackouts, broken promises
  - The VPOP initiative isn't a foreign fix, it is our youth, our money, our action
- Grassroots Ownership
  - Volunteer-based, diaspora-funded security
  - Pilot in Cap-Haïtien has already inspired confidence and early success

- Hope as a Weapon
  - Visible change restores belief
  - "Hope" builds civic momentum gangs can't suppress

- 6.3 Diaspora Makes It Real
  - Budget Reality
    - Haiti's annual security budget: <$100M, half reportedly misused
    - MSS and UN initiatives often stall or lack of transparency
  - Diaspora Potential
    - $4B in remittances = unmatched resources
    - $1M = 200 VPOP volunteers + 15 km² secured
    - Year 2 goal: 1,000 volunteers + 50 km² reclaimed
  - Start Small, Win Fast
    - The VPOP initiative can deliver immediate, measurable impact with modest capital

  - Diaspora-led funding ensures agility and accountability

- 6.4 The VPOP initiative is Ours
  - No Outsiders Needed
    - The VPOP initiative is 100% Haitian-led, no foreign mandates or delays
    - Training, strategy, and leadership rooted in real experience
  - Proven Track Record
    - CAT Team cohorts trained and deployed under Haitian leadership
    - Not theory, done before, can do again
  - Unity in Action
    - Diaspora has kept Haiti alive, now helps fight for it
    - When Haitians unite, gangs lose

- 6.5 Activity Summary
  - Strategic Initiative
    - VPOP = organized community action + law enforcement partnership

- o Initial deployment: 200 VPOP + HNP = foundational shift in local security
- Diaspora Engagement
  - o $1M diaspora investment = real-time change on the ground
  - o Proof-of-concept in Cap-Haïtien ready for national scale-up
- Local Leadership, Lasting Impact
  - o Haitian-run, community-rooted, diaspora-backed
  - o Focused on self-determination, not external dependence
- Scalable Vision
  - o Year 1:200 volunteers/15 km^2
  - o Year 2:1,000 volunteers/50 km^2
- Transformational Potential
  - o A unified VPOP/HNP front reclaims public space
  - o Community trust grows, crime falls, and peace becomes possible
- Final Message

- o The VPOP initiative is not a plan, it's a movement
- o When we lead ourselves, we win

CALL TO ACTION

LOCAL HAITIANS: STEP UP

Cap-Haïtien is the first, with 50 volunteers currently participating and 150 soon to follow. Walk to your commissariat and say, "I'm in." You are 17–35, ready to train, ready to fight, $200/month keeps you going. Tell your pastor, your cousin, your crew, spread it. This city is your home; we must take it back.

The VPOP plan will encourage locals to play a proactive role in improving security within their communities. Cap-Haïtien will serve as the pilot city, with an initial recruitment target of 50 volunteers, which may expand to 150 in the near future.

Individuals within the age range of 17 to 35 can participate by visiting their local police commissariat and committing themselves to join the initiative.

Volunteers will receive $200 per month to help sustain their involvement and dedication to the program. This opportunity will require participants to undergo training and prepare themselves to support the Haitian National Police in its mission to combat crime and restore public safety. Community leaders, such as pastors, cousins, and local influencers, may help spread awareness and encourage broader participation. The program will empower residents to reclaim control over their neighborhoods and contribute to the protection of their shared homes.

HAITIAN DIASPORA: BACK US UP

Pledge today, $100, $500, $1,000, via [to be determined] or email me at [to be determined]. Five dollars a week funds a bullet; $1,000 buys a bond, builds a future. Join our board, watch your money work, contact me at [to be determined]. You are not donors; you are partners.

The Haitian diaspora can play a vital role in strengthening security efforts in Haiti through active financial and strategic support. Members of the diaspora may pledge contributions in amounts ranging from $100 to $1,000 or more, which can help fund essential resources for the VPOP initiative and the Haitian National Police (HNP). A small weekly donation, such as five dollars, could potentially finance critical supplies like equipment or ammunition.

Larger contributions, such as $1,000, may provide bonds that fund long-term stability and institutional growth within the program. These investments will contribute to immediate security needs and help build a foundation for a more secure future in Haiti. Supporters can further engage by joining the program's advisory board, which will allow them to monitor the impact of their contributions actively and provide valuable input. This collaborative approach positions contributors as partners in creating meaningful, sustainable change for Haiti.

NEXT STEPS

May 2025: Training starts, 50 volunteers, Cap-Haïtien.

July 2025: Patrols roll, 200 strong, 15 km^2.

December 2025: Results will be in, crime will be down, trust will be up, and gangs will be out.

The next phase of the VPOP initiative is set to begin in May 2025. Training sessions for 50 selected volunteers will take place in Cap-Haïtien. This program will aim to enhance public safety and bolster the operational capacity of the Haitian National Police. Participants will receive focused instruction to prepare them for community engagement and security support roles. The initiative may create stronger ties between local communities and law enforcement. By deploying trained volunteers, the VPOP plan can contribute to addressing critical security challenges in Haiti.

By July 2025, the VPOP initiative will deploy 200 trained personnel to conduct patrols across a designated 15 square kilometer area in Haiti. This initiative will reinforce security measures and strengthen partnerships with the Haitian National Police. The presence of VPOP officers will deter criminal activity and improve public safety in key regions.

The VPOP staff members may also assist in gathering intelligence to support targeted operations led by national authorities. These patrols will establish a consistent security presence that can help stabilize vulnerable areas. The program will contribute to restoring a sense of order and trust within local communities.

By December 2025, the VPOP initiative could lead to significant improvements in Haiti's security landscape. Crime rates may decrease as trained volunteer officers strengthen the operational capacity of the Haitian National Police. The program could foster renewed trust between law enforcement and local communities through consistent engagement and visible accountability. Organized gangs may face greater resistance due to enhanced police presence and collaborative efforts to dismantle criminal networks. These outcomes will reflect the program's potential to combat lawlessness and restore public confidence in security institutions. See the image below.

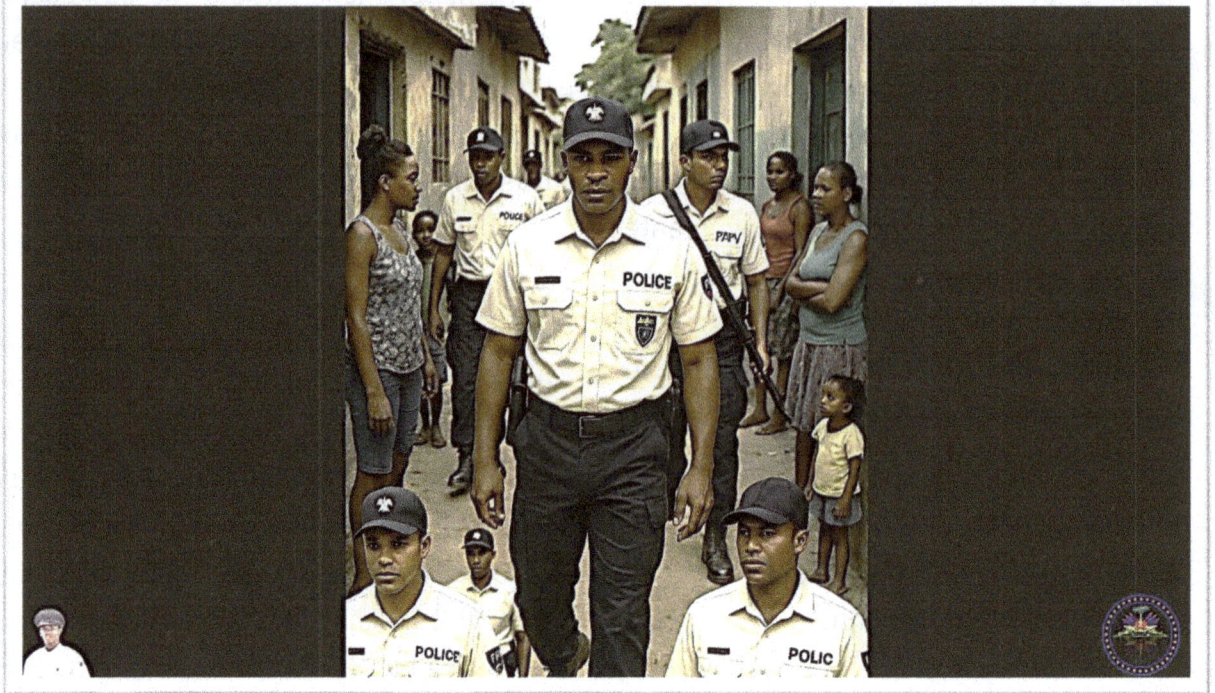

I will be heading to DC soon, pitching MSS and U.S. brass, $1M from you, $1M from them, Cap-Haïtien's ours in nine months. But it starts with us, Haitians, home and away.

The VPOP initiative could provide crucial support in improving security in Haiti by collaborating closely with the Haitian National Police (HNP). This initiative may create opportunities for Haitians, both domestic and diaspora, to contribute to restoring stability actively. A combined commitment of resources from international partners and Haitian leadership might encourage faster implementation and scaling of the program. A financial investment of $1 million from local sponsors and an equivalent commitment from international allies could potentially secure stabilization efforts in regions like Cap-Haïtien within nine months. At its core, the program will rely on the dedication and unity of Haitians to achieve tangible results on the ground. See the image below.

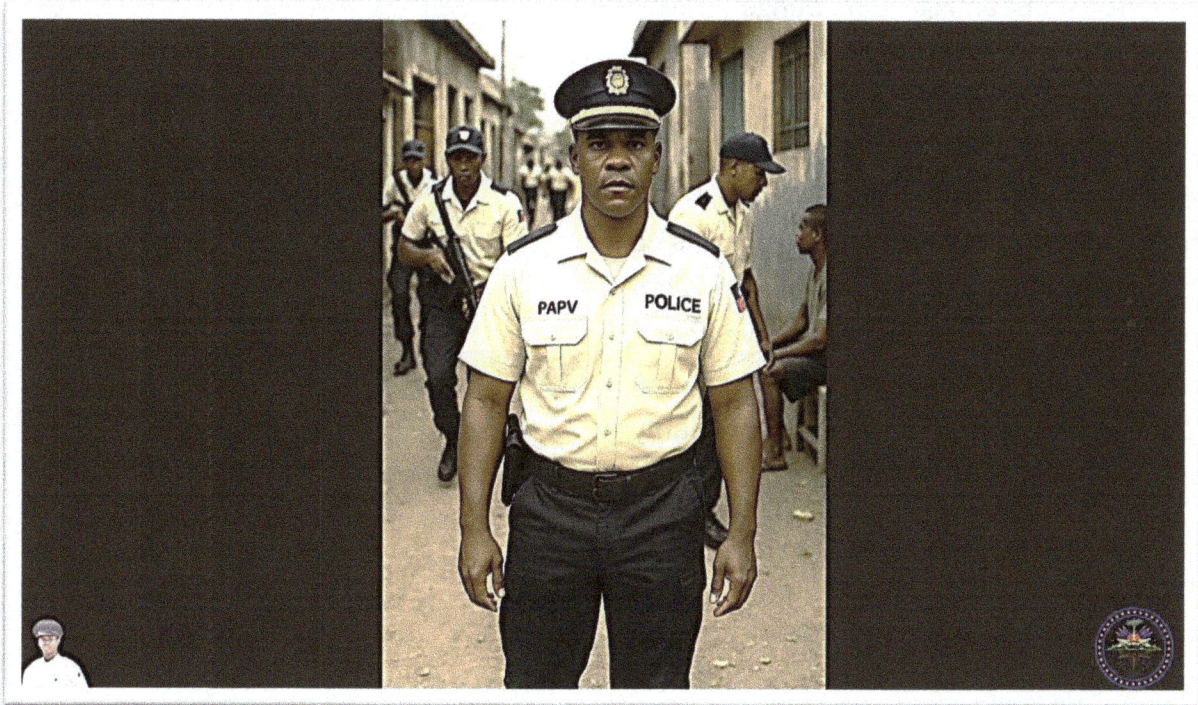

ACTIVITY SUMMARY

The power to reclaim security and stability in Haiti lies within the hands of its people. Local residents are encouraged to take proactive steps by joining the VPOP initiative, actively participating in their community's safety initiatives. Their involvement can create a ripple effect of change, with training and support ensuring that they are well equipped to confront the challenges facing their neighborhoods.

The Haitian diaspora possesses a unique opportunity to affect real change through financial support and strategic partnerships. By pledging contributions, diaspora members can facilitate essential resources that bolster the efforts of both the VPOP initiative and the Haitian National Police. Their engagement will foster a deeper connection to the homeland and create a sustainable framework for progress.

As the VPOP initiative prepares to launch its initiatives, the anticipated timelines highlight a clear path forward. Training will commence in May 2025, providing the groundwork for significant outcomes by the end of the year. The community's efforts, backed by the diaspora, may lead to tangible improvements in safety, a reduction in crime, and an increase in public trust in law enforcement.

The upcoming meetings with stakeholders in Washington, DC, signify a major step in leveraging external support for local initiatives. The goal of securing $1 million in funding from both local and international sources may serve as a catalyst for meaningful change in Cap-Haïtien and beyond. This collective action will not only enhance security measures but will also foster a sense of solidarity among Haitians everywhere.

The success of the VPOP initiative hinges on the collaboration and commitment of every individual, whether on the ground in Haiti or abroad. Together, Haitians can forge a brighter future, reclaim their communities, and build a legacy of resilience and empowerment. The time to act is now.

RECOMMENDATIONS AND OUTLINE

Below is a structured outline of the section and the ideas proposed here. This outline is specific to this chapter and only includes the main points and arguments.

Introduction: The Vision" and "Activity Summary"

- 7. Call to Action (Outline)
- 7.1 Local Haitians: Step Up
    - Pilot City: Cap-Haïtien

- 50 volunteers are already engaged: 150 more expected
- Ages 17–35 eligible to apply at local police commissariats

- Compensation & Commitment
    - $200/month stipend supports volunteer sustainability
    - Volunteers undergo training and serve alongside Haitian National Police (HNP)

- Community Engagement
    - Encourage participation through word-of-mouth, pastors, friends, and families
    - Emphasis on local ownership: "This city is your home; take it back."

- Outcome
    - Residents become protectors of their own neighborhoods
    - Community pride and accountability drive the mission

- 7.2 Haitian Diaspora: Back Us Up
  - Contribution Opportunities
    - Pledge options: $100, $500, $1,000+
    - Donations fund gear, logistics, and training: e.g., $5/week funds a bullet; $1,000 builds operational capacity
  - Strategic Involvement
    - Diaspora invited to join advisory board for visibility and governance
    - Emphasizes partnership, not charity, diaspora are co-owners of the solution
  - Impact
    - Small recurring donations = large, sustained support network
    - Diaspora investment ensures faster deployment and deeper impact

- Implementation Timeline
  - May 2025: Training begins for the first 50 volunteers in Cap-Haïtien
  - July 2025: Deployment of 200 personnel across 15 km² area
  - December 2025: Anticipated results, reduced crime, restored trust, gang retreat
- Operational Strategy
  - Volunteers support HNP patrols, community engagement, and intel gathering
  - Goals: establish consistent security presence, rebuild public trust, stabilize territory
- Strategic Partnerships
  - Outreach to MSS, U.S. partners in Washington, DC
  - Goal: $1M from diaspora + $1M from allies = full Cap-Haïtien rollout in 9 months
- Message
  - "It starts with us," mobilizing Haitians at home and abroad to lead the change

- 7.3 Next Steps

- 7.4 Activity Summary
- Local Engagement
    - Haitians on the ground play a leading role in reclaiming security
    - The VPOP initiative offers structured training and support for effective action
- Diaspora Empowerment
    - Strategic and financial backing turns vision into reality
    - Strengthens emotional and economic ties with the homeland
- Clear Milestones
    - May to December 2025 provides a measurable path forward
    - Training → Deployment → Impact
- National and Global Unity
    - U.S. and MSS partnerships multiply impact, but local leadership remains central
    - Emphasizes Haitian-led solutions to Haitian problems
- Unified Vision
    - The VPOP effort hinges on collaboration, courage, and commitment
    - A resilient, united Haitian people can dismantle gangs, restore order, and build a lasting legacy of peace
- Final Note
    - The time to act is now, security begins with solidarity

THE BIGGER PICTURE

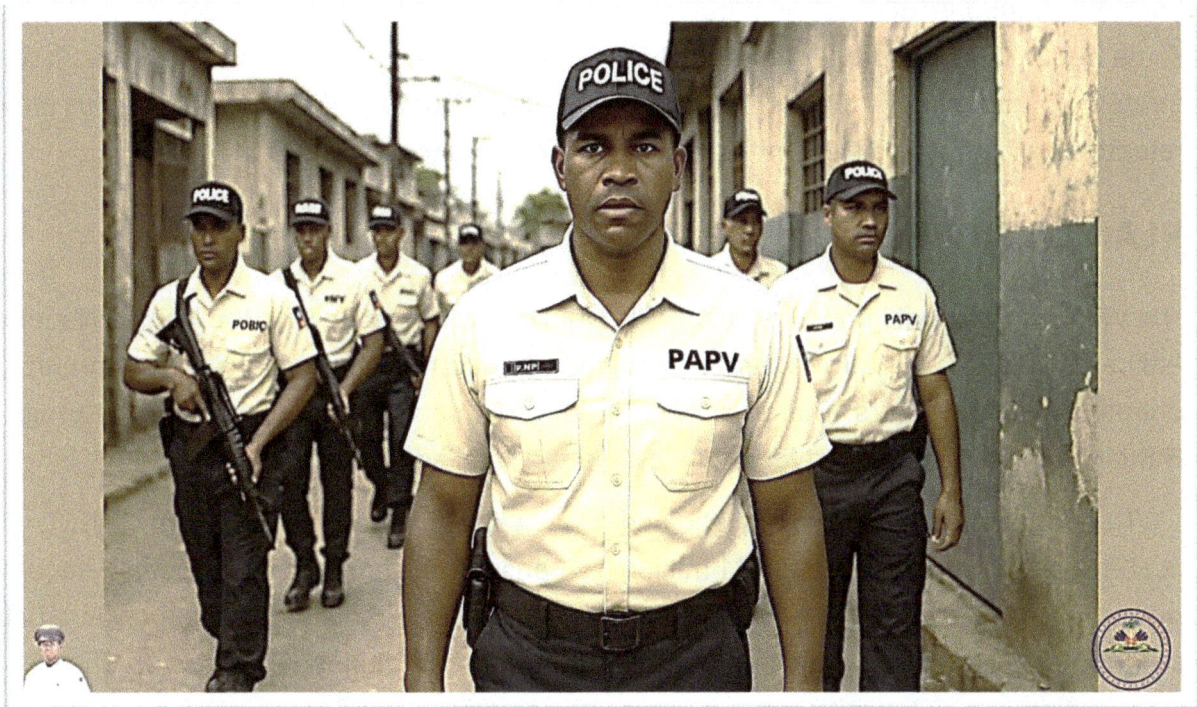

VPOP's not the end, it is the spark. My PPDS has five phases, PPD-1 (this pilot) to PPD-5 (normalization). Cap-Haïtien's 15 km² is step one; Port-au-Prince's 80% gang zone is the prize. The VPOP initiative feeds PNS, 200 now, 2,000 later, funded by you, scaled by us. Gangs do not sleep; neither will we.

The VPOP initiative represents a starting point rather than a conclusion. It aims to ignite progress in enhancing security and restoring order in Haiti. The program is structured into five distinct phases, ranging from the pilot phase, PPD-1, to the final phase, PPD-5, which focuses on full normalization of security operations. The initial implementation will target Cap-Haïtien, an area spanning 15 square kilometers. Future expansion may address larger and more complex regions, including the heavily gang-controlled zones of Port-au-Prince.

The VPOP initiative will contribute to the growth of the Haitian National Police Support (PNS) network by recruiting and training security personnel. The program currently supports 200 officers but may scale to 2,000 with proper funding and strategic planning. Gangs operate relentlessly, and The VPOP initiative will match their determination to improve safety within these communities.

This is personal. I joined the HNP in '95 to serve Haiti, trained in the U.S. to learn how, and came back because I cannot stay away. Our youth deserves streets, not graves; our diaspora deserves pride, not pity. The VPOP initiative is "Fòs Nou, Espwa Nou," Our Strength, Our Hope. Let us move forward for a better Haiti.

PLAN OVERVIEW

The VPOP initiative will enhance security in Haiti by collaborating with the Haitian National Police (HNP). This initiative aims to strengthen public trust through visible, community-oriented policing efforts. Diaspora engagement will serve as a cornerstone, leveraging Haitian communities abroad for funding, expertise, and advocacy.

The program will prioritize realistic and scalable solutions with an initial $1 million budget supported by diaspora contributions. By piloting the program in Cap-Haïtien, the VPOP initiative will focus on a manageable, high-impact area to ensure measurable results. This localized approach will allow for responsive adjustments before expanding nationwide.

Clear coordination with HNP will ensure alignment with existing security strategies. This approach will help reinforce sustainable outcomes. The VPOP initiative can serve as a model of innovation and collaboration in addressing Haiti's pressing security needs.

IMPORTANT NOTES

Plan Length: The plan is short, detailed but easily digestible.

Plan Goals: Mirror a quick response initiative, vision to action, diaspora heavy.

Plan Urgency Tone: Direct, personal, urgent, rooted in the author's HNP/CAT Team credentials.

Plan Funding: $1M diaspora ask, lean and realistic (based on PPD strategic document).

Plan Location [Cap-Haïtien]: Specific, winnable, and pilot-ready.

I became a police officer to make a difference in my country. I sought training in the United States to enhance my skills and bring them back to Haiti. Returning home was never a question in my mind because my commitment to Haiti runs deep.

The youth of our nation deserve safe streets where they can dream, not graves marked by violence. The diaspora deserves to feel pride in their homeland, not pity for its struggles. The motto "Fòs Nou, Espwa Nou" embodies our mission. Together, we can take action; we can restore hope; we can rebuild strength for a safer and brighter Haiti.

ACTIVITY SUMMARY

The VPOP initiative represents a critical turning point for enhancing security in Haiti. It offers a structured pathway that builds on the initial success in Cap-Haïtien and sets the stage for future expansions into more challenging regions, predominantly in Port-au-Prince. By focusing on community-oriented policing, the program aims to foster public trust and engagement. The partnership with the Haitian National Police will ensure that our approach aligns with national security strategies.

Engagement with the diaspora will be pivotal in attracting necessary resources and expertise. The initial budget may indeed prove sufficient for launching the pilot in Cap-Haïtien, but as the program scales to accommodate 2,000 officers [potentially], additional funding will be essential. Highlights of our initiative will remain its adaptability and focus on measurable outcomes, ensuring that any adjustments made in response to initial challenges will lay the groundwork for comprehensive reforms.

This endeavor transcends mere policy; it is deeply personal and rooted in a shared commitment to the future of Haiti. Every step taken will reflect our collective involvement and dedication. The VPOP initiative is not just a plan but a movement, one that seeks accountability, restoration, and hope for the youth of our nation. As we move forward, let us uphold the spirit of "Fòs Nou, Espwa Nou," our strength and our hope, guiding us toward a more secure and vibrant Haiti.

RECOMMENDATIONS AND OUTLINE

Below is a structured outline of the section and the ideas proposed here. This outline is specific to this chapter and only includes the main points and arguments.

Introduction: The Vision" and "Activity Summary"

- 8. The Bigger Picture (Outline)
  - 8.1 Strategic Vision: From Spark to System
    - Phased Roadmap: PPD-1 to PPD-5
      - PPD-1: The VPOP initiative pilot in Cap-Haïtien (15 km²)
      - PPD-5: Full normalization of law and order across Haiti
      - Long-term goal: reclaim Port-au-Prince, where gangs control ~80% of the territory
    - Scalable Growth
      - The VPOP initiative currently supports 200 personnel
      - Target: expand to 2,000 officers with proper funding and diaspora support
    - Integration with PNS (Police Nationale/National Police Support)
      - The VPOP initiative is designed to feed talent, structure, and operational support into the broader HNP ecosystem
      - Reinforces national policing capacity from the ground up
  - Moral Imperative
    - Founder's background: joined HNP in 1995, trained in the U.S., returned to serve Haiti
    - Mission driven by urgency: "Our youth deserve streets, not graves; our diaspora deserves pride, not pity."
    - Motto: "Fòs Nou, Espwa Nou:" Our Strength, Our Hope

- 8.1.1 Plan Overview
- Partnership with HNP
  - Coordination ensures alignment with national security strategies
  - Strengthens legitimacy and operational reach of local policing efforts
- Diaspora as Keystone
  - Funding, expertise, advocacy driven by Haitian communities abroad

- o Diaspora positioned as strategic investors, not just donors
- Lean and Focused Launch
  - o Budget: $1M diaspora-driven seed capital
  - o Target: Cap-Haïtien, a controlled, winnable testbed for larger replication
- Local-First Strategy
  - o Measurable outcomes before national scale
  - o Iterative feedback loop for continuous improvement
- Innovation and Realism
  - o Combines urgency with practicality
  - o Designed to produce fast, visible wins while laying groundwork for structural reform

---

- 8.1.2 Key Planning Notes
- Plan Length: Concise, focused, and accessible
- Plan Goals: Rapid-response structure with diaspora collaboration at its core
- Tone: Direct, urgent, and personal, draws from the author's law enforcement experience

- Plan Funding: Lean $1M target based on scalable PPD blueprint
- Plan Location: Cap-Haïtien chosen for its strategic feasibility and high impact potential

---

- 8.2 Activity Summary
- Pilot as Catalyst
  - o Cap-Haïtien serves as a foundational proof of concept
  - o Results will inform expansion into Port-au-Prince and other high-risk areas
- Community Policing at the Core
  - o Builds public trust through daily engagement and accountability
  - o Shifts policing from distant authority to neighborhood partnership
- Diaspora-Driven Sustainability
  - o Financial contributions and governance input from abroad enable growth
  - o Diaspora engagement connects global resources to local needs
- Funding Path Forward

- o Initial $1M covers pilot phase
- o Scaling to 2,000 officers will require expanded investment and international partnership

- Commitment Over Policy
  - o This is more than a proposal, it's a mission grounded in personal sacrifice and national pride
  - o Reflects a collective promise to rebuild safety, dignity, and hope for Haiti's future

- Guiding Ethos
  - o "Fòs Nou, Espwa Nou" is not just a slogan, it is the movement's foundation
  - o Haitians at home and abroad united in restoring their homeland

RECLAIMING HAITI BACK

Haiti finds itself at a pivotal juncture. For too long, we have been a nation defined by what we have lost, territory to gangs, trust to corruption, and hope to despair. The paralysis gripping us as of May 2025 is not just a failure of leadership or resources; it is a failure of will. But I believe in us, in the grit of our youth, the strength of our diaspora, and the unyielding spirit that has carried Haiti through centuries of struggle.

The Voluntary Police Officer Program- The VPOP initiative is more than a plan; it is a declaration that we will not surrender our country to chaos. It is a call to action rooted in a truth I have learned over three decades of service: numbers win fights, and hope wins futures.

This document lays out a clear path, 200 volunteers, trained under my watch, will be deployed in Cap-Haïtien to reclaim 15 square kilometers from the grip of fear. It is not a grand invasion of Port-au-Prince or a foreign-led rescue; it is a Haitian start, small enough to succeed, big enough to matter.

The Principle of Numerical Superiority (PNS), the backbone of my broader Police Presence Deployment Strategy (PPDS), demands that we outmatch our enemies, 3-to-1, 4-to-1, whatever it takes. The VPOP initiative delivers that edge, not with empty promises or borrowed boots, but with our hands, youth stepping up at home, diaspora stepping in from abroad.

The diaspora plays a crucial role in this endeavor. Your $4 billion in yearly remittances has kept Haiti alive; now, $1 million can help us fight. This project is not about charity; it is about partnership.

Crowdfunding and VPOP Bonds put the power in your hands, with every dollar tracked, every patrol filmed, and every victory shared. I have lived among you, studied in your universities, and trained in your bases; I know the longing you carry for a Haiti that stands tall. The VPOP initiative is your chance to turn that longing into action, to fund a force that does not just protect but rebuild. Together, we will prove that Haiti's salvation does not wait on Port-au-Prince's politicians or the UN's timelines, it begins where we decide it does.

Cap-Haïtien is our proving ground. With 450,000 people, a moderate crime rate, and a police force ready for reinforcement, it is the right place to break the current state of paralysis. Using my experience from Fort Leonard Wood and the CAT Team, we will transform 200 volunteers into a unit capable of accurate shooting, clean arrests, and active listening within six weeks of training.

In six months of deployment, backed by seven teams and diaspora-funded gear, we will cut crime by 20%, lift trust to 70%, and send gangs running from 15 km^2. These are not guesses; they are targets, measurable by HNP logs, civilian voices, and MSS eyes. Success here is not the end of it all; it is the spark. From Cap-Haïtien, we will scale to Jacmel, to Léogâne, and to the ganglands of Port-au-Prince. Each step will be fueled by more volunteers, more diaspora dollars, and more hope.

The subject is personal for me. I joined the HNP in 1995 as part of its first wave. I was trained both in the U.S. and in Haiti. I learned to defend my country. I led the CAT Team because I believed we could be more than a battered force.

Early on, I left the police when corruption choked my dream to serve the homeland. However, Haiti has always remained in my heart. Now, after years abroad, studying, teaching, watching our nation's fray, I am back with a plan born from experience, not a theory. The VPOP initiative is not just my idea; it is our idea. My friends heard it in my voice this week; hope was stirring in my voice, as they heard my cries for a chance to fight; they felt it too. That is the power of us, not just me. This is a matter that concerns Haitians at home and in the diaspora. The diaspora can encourage volunteerism, invest in their courage, and have faith in their determination to save Haiti.

The VPOP initiative is not flawless. The risks are real. Gangs will not sit quietly and wait for us. They will push back undoubtedly. They will test us; they may even strike early. Corruption could creep in, trust could waver, and funds could falter. But I have faced ambushes before; I have trained men to hold the lines; I have seen communities rally when given a reason to do so. The guardrails of VPOP, which include local leaders' vetting, diaspora oversight, and my personal presence on the ground, will ensure its stability. We can start to learn. We can prove that the VPOP initiative works. We can adjust where it bends. This is not blind optimism; it is calculated to resolve.

The bigger picture looms beyond Cap-Haïtien. My PPDS envisions five phases, PPD-1's pilot growing into PPD-5's nationwide peace. The VPOP initiative is the seed, with 200 volunteers today, 2,000 tomorrow, and a revitalized HNP that not only patrols but also governs the land. The diaspora's $1 million is the first drop; with success, MSS and U.S. funds will flow, turning a Haitian spark into a national fire. Gangs thrive in our weakness; we will bury them with our strength. See the image below.

"Fòs Nou, Espwa Nou," Our Strength, Our Hope. That's VPOP's promise. To the youth of Cap-Haïtien: your courage will kick-start this initiative. To the diaspora:

your dollars will fuel it. To Haiti: Your future waits on us.

The plan is to head to Washington and New York in the coming days or weeks to discuss this initiative with the relevant stakeholders. The goal is to pitch this campaign to embassies with the voices of the Haitian Diaspora behind me. With $1M from us (diaspora) and $1M from them, we can reclaim Cap-Haïtien in nine months. But it does not need their nod to begin, it needs ours.

RECOMMENDATIONS AND OUTLINE

Below is a structured outline of the section and the ideas proposed here. This outline is specific to this chapter and only includes the main points and arguments.

Introduction: The Vision" and "Activity Summary"

- 9. Reclaiming Haiti Back (Outline)
- 9.1 National Context & Moral Imperative
- Crisis Overview
  - o Haiti is at a pivotal crossroads, crippled by gang control, institutional distrust, and societal despair

  - o The core issue is not just lack of leadership or resources, but a failure of will
- Foundational Belief
  - o A deep belief in Haiti's potential: the resolve of its youth, the strength of its diaspora, and the spirit of its people
  - o The VPOP initiative is a declaration of refusal to surrender Haiti to lawlessness
- Guiding Truth
  - o Grounded in three decades of policing: "Numbers win fights. Hope wins futures."

- 9.2 Program Launch & Tactical Focus
- Initial Deployment
  - o 200 trained volunteers deployed in Cap-Haïtien
  - o 15 km^2 area targeted for security reclamation
- Local-Led Strategy
  - o No foreign military or UN presence; this is a Haitian-led, Haitian-grown initiative

- o Designed to be "small enough to succeed, big enough to matter."

- Tactical Doctrine

  - o Based on the Principle of Numerical Superiority (PNS), outnumbering threats 3:1 or more

  - o Strategy feeds into broader Police Presence Deployment Strategy (PPDS)

- 9.3 Diaspora as Force Multiplier

- Financial Role

  - o Diaspora contributes $4B annually in remittances

  - o Now, $1M is asked, not as charity, but as an investment in security and hope

- Mechanisms

  - o Crowdfunding & VPOP Bonds for transparency and community participation

  - o Full accountability: dollars tracked, patrols recorded, progress shared

- Emotional Connection

  - o Diaspora's longing for a proud, safe Haiti channeled into actionable support

- o The VPOP initiative is a chance to turn emotion into empowerment

---

- 9.4 Cap-Haïtien: The Proving Ground

- Why Cap-Haïtien?

  - o Population: ~450,000

  - o Moderate crime rate; police receptive to reinforcement

  - o Strategic location to demonstrate model success

- Training & Deployment Goals

  - o 6 weeks of training: firearms, arrest protocol, de-escalation, and community engagement

  - o 6 months of operations: 7 teams, diaspora-funded gear

- Measurable Targets

  - o Reduce crime by 20%

  - o Raise trust in police to 70%

  - o Reclaim 15 km^2 from gang control

  - o Metrics via HNP logs, community feedback, and MSS oversight

---

- 9.5 Personal Commitment & Leadership
- Author's Background
  - HNP founding cohort (1995), U.S. and Haiti-trained
  - Led CAT Team; resigned due to corruption but never lost resolve
- Return with Purpose
  - After years abroad, educating, observing, and organizing, returning with a practical plan, not a theory
  - Reengagement driven by moral obligation and professional confidence
- Shared Ownership
  - Initiative shaped by shared voices: "This is not just my plan, it is our plan."
  - Diaspora can foster pride and participation by backing volunteer courage

---

- 9.6 Risks, Guardrails, and Resilience
- Acknowledged Risks
  - Gang retaliation, corruption, wavering trust, funding volatility
- Mitigation Measures

- Local leader vetting
- Diaspora financial oversight
- On-the-ground leadership presence by the program founder
- Philosophy of Adaptability
  - The VPOP initiative is not presented as flawless, it is resilient and adjustable
  - "This is not blind optimism; it is calculated to resolve."

- 9.7 Scaling Up: From Spark to Strategy
- PPDS Framework
  - Five-phase strategy from pilot (PPD-1) to national normalization (PPD-5)
  - Pathway: Cap-Haïtien → Jacmel → Léogâne → Port-au-Prince
- Growth Metrics
  - From 200 volunteers to 2,000 across the nation
  - Transition from patrol support to full-governance capacity
- Future Funding
  - Initial diaspora-led investment ($1M) to be

matched by international funds (MSS, U.S. sources)

- o Proof of the concept will trigger further resource mobilization

---

- 9.8 Call to Action
- To the Youth of Haiti: Your courage launches the mission
- To the Diaspora: Your $1M fuels it, your faith sustains it
- To the Nation: "Your future waits on us, not on politicians or the UN."
- Immediate Next Steps
  - o U.S. advocacy: upcoming visits to Washington and New York
  - o Goal: pitch The VPOP initiative to embassies, secure diaspora and diplomatic backing
- Final Note
  - o "Fòs Nou, Espwa Nou, Our Strength, Our Hope" is more than a motto, it's the foundation
  - o Reclaiming Cap-Haïtien is only the beginning. It starts with our will, not their permission

The Voluntary Police Officer Program (VPOP)

FINAL THOUGHTS

Haiti stands at a critical turning point, where the challenge presents an opportunity for transformation. The pervasive struggles of the past cannot define our future. Our collective determination, fueled by the resilience of our youth and the commitment of our diaspora, can change the narrative. The Voluntary Police Officer Program (VPOP) embodies this potential. It represents a decisive shift from despair to action, moving towards tangible outcomes instead of abstract hopes.

The strategic deployment of trained volunteers in Cap-Haïtien will serve as a model for reclaiming safety and trust. A commitment of 200 volunteers is not merely an ambitious target; it is a promise of progress in a community that deserves to flourish. Establishing a clear framework, including the Principle of Numerical Superiority, will enhance our ability to confront and outmatch criminal elements effectively.

Active participation from the diaspora will prove vital. Your financial contributions can amplify our efforts, transforming resources into meaningful action. The

VPOP initiative is not only a project but a partnership that allows a shared vision for a safe and vibrant Haiti. Together, we will cultivate a culture of accountability and success, driven by transparency and community involvement.

While the challenges ahead are significant, the path laid out is one of hope and resilience. The risks associated with the implementation of the VPOP initiative are acknowledged, yet our determination will counteract these potential setbacks. Through community support and oversight, we can adapt and refine our approach as necessary.

The vision extends beyond Cap-Haïtien. Each success will pave the way for a broader initiative across Haiti, where our commitment will lead to heightened safety and governance. The potential impact of the VPOP initiative will ignite a new era of cooperation amongst all Haitians, fostering a renewed sense of pride in our homeland.

Haiti stands at a defining crossroads; one where deep-rooted challenges can give way to a new era of transformation. The hardships and instability that have marked our past must no longer dictate our future. Instead, we are called to act, drawing strength from the resilience of our youth and the enduring commitment of our diaspora. The Voluntary Police Officer Program (VPOP) is not just a response to our security crisis; it is a movement grounded in purpose and possibility. It marks the shift from abstract hope to concrete action, a chance to begin reclaiming what has been lost with a plan that is measurable, inclusive, and Haitian-led.

The pilot deployment of 200 trained volunteers in Cap-Haïtien is more than a tactical maneuver, it is a promise to restore security, dignity, and public trust. This localized intervention, supported by the Principle of Numerical Superiority, offers a scalable framework to outmatch and outlast the criminal forces threatening our communities. This approach is grounded in the belief that safety and hope must walk hand in hand, and that we can win when we organize, train, and lead with purpose.

The role of the Haitian diaspora in this effort cannot be overstated. Your contributions, be they financial, professional, and emotional, are not acts of charity but of solidarity. The VPOP initiative offers a mechanism for partnership: every dollar raised, every patrol documented, and every community impacted will reflect our shared ownership of Haiti's future. This is an opportunity to transform diaspora engagement into a powerful force for national renewal, building a culture of accountability, transparency, and local empowerment.

We recognize that the path forward will not be without risk. Gangs will resist, systems may falter, and unforeseen challenges will arise. Yet, our resolve is stronger. With community oversight, real-time adaptability, and grounded leadership, the VPOP initiative can withstand pressure and evolve when necessary. The early wins in Cap-Haïtien will be our foundation, not our ceiling, each milestone laying the groundwork for broader expansion across the country.

The success of the VPOP initiative will help ignite a wider movement toward national restoration, one that spans from Cap-Haïtien to Port-au-Prince and beyond. It is a vision for a Haiti where communities are protected, youth are empowered, and the state regains its rightful role as a provider of safety and stability. The momentum begins now, with those willing to step forward, contribute, and believe that reclaiming Haiti is not a dream but a duty.

To all Haitians, at home and abroad, this is your call to action. The urgency is real. Therefore, the time for action is now. Whether by volunteering, donating, sharing the vision, or simply standing with us, your participation is vital.

Let this be the moment we choose to rise as a nation and as a people. Haiti has a long tradition of pride. However, the country has slipped out of destiny's favor. Let this be the step that begins the journey back to where we belong. Let us rebuild Haiti by reclaiming one city at a time from violent gangs. Let us reclaim our nation with one voice at a time and by claiming one victory at a time.

I understand that reclaiming Haiti is a collective endeavor. I need your support; Haiti needs your support. Let us build an alliance for the motherland. We waited long enough. It is time to take Haiti back from criminal gangsters.

Haitians, both local and abroad, must embrace this moment. The urgency of our situation calls for immediate action. By stepping forward, each of us can contribute to a brighter future for Haiti, where strength and hope converge. Let us unite our efforts, share this mission, and work hand in hand to reclaim our country for generations to come.

We invite all Haitians, whether at home or abroad, to join us in this urgent initiative to reclaim our beloved nation. Your support is crucial. There are many ways to get involved.

Whether you choose to volunteer, donate, or simply spread the word, each action contributes to our shared vision for a safer and more prosperous Haiti. You can sign up for updates, pledge your support so we can keep you informed about our progress and upcoming opportunities to engage.

You can help spread this plan to those who might be losing hope for peace and security in the homeland.

Haiti is dying little by little. Let us not wait any longer. The time for action is now. To learn how you can make a difference, please reach out to us directly through [mygen70@gmail.com].

A Peaceful and Prosperous Haiti is Possible—Dr. Ben Wood Johnson (August 2025)

INDEX

ABOUT THE AUTHOR

Ben Wood Johnson, Ph.D.

EXPERTISE & EXPERIENCE

Ben Wood Johnson, Ph.D., is an accomplished security expert and a dedicated professional within the Haitian National Police. With a distinguished professional background and academic career, which spans over 30 years, Dr. Johnson has made significant contributions to the field of policing and national security. His initial contribution started in 1997 when he helped design the Haitian National Palace Safety and Security Plans (Alpha, Bravo, and Charly Plans). Dr. Johnson also helped establish the security parameters for the Haitian National Police in 2006. His involvement in Haitian security matters extends all the way into the year 2025, with the original document you hold in your hands being transmitted to Haitian officials in 2024. The original version of the document had been drafted specifically for the General Director of the Haitian National Police.

PROFESSIONAL EXPERIENCE

Commander of the Counter Ambush and Terrorism Team (CAT Team): Dr. Johnson served as the Commander of the CAT Team, where he led efforts to combat terrorism and ambush threats, thereby ensuring the safety and security of the nation.

Leadership Roles: Throughout his career, Dr. Johnson has held several leadership positions, including in the Anti-riot Police Unit (CIMO), the SWAT Team, and the Presidential Security Unit (PSU).

ACADEMIC BACKGROUND

Dr. Johnson holds a doctorate in educational administration and leadership. He has studied other fields, including, but not limited to, politics, public administration, law, ethics, and criminal justice. Dr. Johnson is a specialist in policing and security and has taught Policing in America.

Dr. Johnson's experience and academic background have equipped him with a deep understanding of the complex security challenges facing Haiti. He is committed to developing and implementing effective strategies to enhance national security and promote stability within the region.

CONTACT INFORMATION

For further information or inquiries, please contact:

Ben Wood Johnson, Ph.D.

Ben Wood Educational Consulting (BWEC, LLC)

Email: Mygen70@gmail.com

ALL RIGHTS RESERVED

ISBN -13: 978-1-948600-92-7

ISBN-10: 1-948600-92-7

For permission and other inquiries, please contact:

X-Ean Prime, Runedan, and Benjamin W. Johnson
Ben Wood Educational Consulting (BWEC, LLC)

330 W. Main St., Unit 214
Middletown, PA 17057

AUTHOR'S NOTE

This document is NOT final. It is still subject to modifications and other alterations, such as content editing or the inclusion/exclusion of other pertinent [or otherwise unnecessary] information. The ideas echoed in this document are based on academic research, personal experience, and other research tools. The views expressed here are authentic and professional in nature. The author does not condone any misuse of the present edition in terms of the PPD document itself [a part thereof or as a whole] or aspects of the techniques, tactics, or strategies contained herein. Any misuse of the ideas or the views expressed in this document is the personal responsibility of the perpetrator.

Leadership-Specific Usage Rights:

Photo Credits

SELECTED WORKS BY BEN WOOD JOHNSON

- ✓ Sartrean Ethics: A Defense of Jean-Paul Sartre as a Moral Philosopher
- ✓ Jean-Paul Sartre and Morality: A Legacy Under Attack
- ✓ Sartre lives on
- ✓ Forced Out of Vietnam: A Policy Analysis of the Fall of Saigon
- ✓ Natural Law: Morality and Obedience
- ✓ Cogito, Ergo Philosophus
- ✓ International Law: The Rise of Russia as a Global Threat
- ✓ Citizen Obedience: The Nature of Legal Obligation
- ✓ Jean-Jacques Rousseau: A Collection of Short Essays
- ✓ Pennsylvania Inspired Leadership: A Roadmap for American Educators
- ✓ Adult Education in America: A Policy Assessment of Adult Learning
- ✓ Striking to Survive: The Human Migration Story
- ✓ Postcolonial Africa: Africa Three Comparative Essays on the African State
- ✓ Go Back Where You Came From
- ✓ Racism: What is it?
- ✓ Discourse on Human Freedom

The Voluntary Police Officer Program (VPOP)

The Voluntary Police Officer Program (VPOP)

www.ingramcontent.com/pod-product-compliance
Lightning Source LLC
Chambersburg PA
CBHW080253030426
42334CB00023BA/2808